I0009441

<u>Disclaimer</u>

Book Title: Cloud Computing Synopsis and Recommendations

Book Author: Mark L. Badger; Timothy Grance; Robert Patt-Corner; Jeffrey M. Voas

Book Abstract: This document reprises the NIST-established definition of cloud computing, describes cloud computing benefits and open issues, presents an overview of major classes of cloud technology, and provides guidelines and recommendations on how organizations should consider the relative opportunities and risks of cloud computing.

Citation: NIST SP - 800-146

Keyword: cloud computing; computer security; virtualization

National Institute of Standards and Technology

U.S. Department of Commerce

Special Publication 800-146

Cloud Computing Synopsis and Recommendations

Recommendations of the National Institute of Standards and Technology

Lee Badger
Tim Grance
Robert Patt-Corner
Jeff Voas

NIST Special Publication 800-146

Cloud Computing Synopsis and Recommendations

Recommendations of the National Institute of Standards and Technology

Lee Badger
Tim Grance
Robert Patt-Corner
Jeff Voas

C O M P U T E R   S E C U R I T Y

Computer Security Division
Information Technology Laboratory
National Institute of Standards and Technology
Gaithersburg, MD 20899-8930

May 2012

U.S. Department of Commerce

John Bryson, Secretary

National Institute of Standards and Technology

Patrick D. Gallagher, Under Secretary of Commerce for
Standards and Technology and Director

Reports on Computer Systems Technology

The Information Technology Laboratory (ITL) at the National Institute of Standards and Technology (NIST) promotes the U.S. economy and public welfare by providing technical leadership for the nation's measurement and standards infrastructure. ITL develops tests, test methods, reference data, proof of concept implementations, and technical analysis to advance the development and productive use of information technology. ITL's responsibilities include the development of management, administrative, technical, and physical standards and guidelines for the cost-effective security and privacy of other than national security-related information in Federal information systems. This Special Publication 800-series reports on ITL's research, guidance, and outreach efforts in computer security and its collaborative activities with industry, government, and academic organizations.

National Institute of Standards and Technology Special Publication 800-146
Natl. Inst. Stand. Technol. Spec. Publ. 800-146, 81 pages (May 2012)

Acknowledgments

The authors, Lee Badger of the National Institute of Standards and Technology (NIST), Tim Grance, of the National Institute of Standards and Technology (NIST), Robert Patt-Corner of Global Tech, Inc., and Jeff Voas of the National Institute of Standards and Technology (NIST), wish to thank their colleagues who reviewed drafts of this document and contributed to its technical content. The authors gratefully acknowledge and appreciate the contributions from individuals and organizations whose comments improved the overall quality of this publication.

Trademark Information

All names are trademarks or registered trademarks of their respective owners.

Table of Contents

List of Figures

List of Tables

List of Appendices

Executive Summary

Cloud computing allows computer users to conveniently rent access to fully featured applications, to software development and deployment environments, and to computing infrastructure assets such as network-accessible data storage and processing.

This document reprises the NIST-established definition of cloud computing, describes cloud computing benefits and open issues, presents an overview of major classes of cloud technology, and provides guidelines and recommendations on how organizations should consider the relative opportunities and risks of cloud computing. Cloud computing has been the subject of a great deal of commentary. Attempts to describe cloud computing in general terms, however, have been problematic because cloud computing is not a single kind of system, but instead spans a spectrum of underlying technologies, configuration possibilities, service models, and deployment models. This document describes cloud systems and discusses their strengths and weaknesses.

Depending on an organization's requirements, different technologies and configurations are appropriate. To understand which part of the spectrum of cloud systems is most appropriate for a given need, an organization should consider how clouds can be deployed (deployment models), what kinds of services can be provided to customers (service models), the economic opportunities and risks of using cloud services (economic considerations), the technical characteristics of cloud services such as performance and reliability (operational characteristics), typical terms of service (service level agreements), and the security opportunities and risks (security).

Deployment Models. A cloud computing system may be deployed privately or hosted on the premises of a cloud customer, may be shared among a limited number of trusted partners, may be hosted by a third party, or may be a publically accessible service, i.e., a public cloud. Depending on the kind of cloud deployment, the cloud may have limited private computing resources, or may have access to large quantities of remotely accessed resources. The different deployment models present a number of tradeoffs in how customers can control their resources, and the scale, cost, and availability of resources.

Service Models. A cloud can provide access to software applications such as email or office productivity tools (the Software as a Service, or SaaS, service model), or can provide an environment for customers to use to build and operate their own software (the Platform as a Service, or PaaS, service model), or can provide network access to traditional computing resources such as processing power and storage (the Infrastructure as a Service, or IaaS, service model). The different service models have different strengths and are suitable for different customers and business objectives. Generally, interoperability and portability of customer workloads is more achievable in the IaaS service model because the building blocks of IaaS offerings are relatively well-defined, e.g., network protocols, CPU instruction sets, and legacy device interfaces.

Economic Considerations. In outsourced and public deployment models, cloud computing provides convenient rental of computing resources: users pay service charges while using a service but need not pay large up-front acquisition costs to build a computing infrastructure. The reduction of up-front costs reduces the risks for pilot projects and experimental efforts, thus reducing a barrier to organizational flexibility, or agility. In outsourced and public deployment models, cloud computing also can provide elasticity, that is, the ability for customers to quickly request, receive, and later release as many resources as needed. By using an elastic cloud, customers may be able to avoid excessive costs from over-provisioning, i.e., building enough capacity for peak demand and then not using the capacity in non-peak periods. Whether or not cloud computing reduces overall costs for an organization depends on a careful analysis of all the costs of operation, compliance, and security, including costs to migrate to and, if necessary, migrate from a cloud.

Operational Characteristics. Cloud computing favors applications that can be broken up into small independent parts. Cloud systems generally depend on networking and hence any limitations on networking, such as data import/export bottlenecks or service disruptions, reduce cloud utility, especially for applications that are not tolerant of disruptions.

Service Agreements, including Service Level Agreements. Organizations should understand the terms of the service agreements that define the legal relationships between cloud customers and cloud providers. An organization should understand customer responsibilities, and those of the service provider, before using a cloud service.

Security. Organizations should be aware of the security issues that exist in cloud computing and of applicable NIST publications such as NIST Special Publication (SP) 800-53 "Recommended Security Controls For Federal Information Systems and Organizations." As complex networked systems, clouds are affected by traditional computer and network security issues such as the needs to provide data confidentiality, data integrity, and system availability. By imposing uniform management practices, clouds may be able to improve on some security update and response issues. Clouds, however, also have potential to aggregate an unprecedented quantity and variety of customer data in cloud data centers. This potential vulnerability requires a high degree of confidence and transparency that cloud providers can keep customer data isolated and protected. Also, cloud users and administrators rely heavily on Web browsers, so browser security failures can lead to cloud security breaches. The privacy and security of cloud computing depend primarily on whether the cloud service provider has implemented robust security controls and a sound privacy policy desired by their customers, the visibility that customers have into its performance, and how well it is managed.

Inherently, the move to cloud computing is a business decision in which the business case should consider the relevant factors, some of which include readiness of existing applications for cloud deployment, transition costs and life-cycle costs, maturity of service orientation in existing infrastructure, and other factors including security and privacy requirements.

1. Introduction

1.1 Authority

The National Institute of Standards and Technology (NIST) developed this document in furtherance of its statutory responsibilities under the Federal Information Security Management Act (FISMA) of 2002, Public Law 107-347.

NIST is responsible for developing standards and guidelines, including minimum requirements, for providing adequate information security for all agency operations and assets; but such standards and guidelines shall not apply to national security systems. This guideline is consistent with the requirements of the Office of Management and Budget (OMB) Circular A-130, Section 8b(3), "Securing Agency Information Systems," as analyzed in A-130, Appendix IV: Analysis of Key Sections. Supplemental information is provided in A-130, Appendix III.

This guideline has been prepared for use by Federal agencies. It may be used by nongovernmental organizations on a voluntary basis and is not subject to copyright, though attribution is desired.

Nothing in this document should be taken to contradict standards and guidelines made mandatory and binding on Federal agencies by the Secretary of Commerce under statutory authority, nor should these guidelines be interpreted as altering or superseding the existing authorities of the Secretary of Commerce, Director of the OMB, or any other Federal official.

1.2 Purpose and Scope

The purpose of this document is to explain the cloud computing technology area in plain terms, and to provide recommendations for information technology decision makers.

Cloud computing is a developing area and its ultimate strengths and weakness are not yet fully researched, documented and tested. This document gives recommendations on how and when cloud computing is an appropriate tool, and indicates the limits of current knowledge and areas for future analysis.

1.3 Audience

This publication is intended to serve a diverse enterprise audience of information systems professionals including chief information officers, information systems developers, project managers, system designers, systems programmers, application programmers, system and network administrators, information system security officers, and system owners.

1.4 Document Structure

The remainder of this document is organized into the following major sections:

- Section 2 reprises the NIST definition of cloud computing.

- Section 3 surveys typical commercial terms of usage for cloud computing systems.

- Section 4 provides a breakdown of how cloud computing solutions may be deployed and describes general implications for different deployment options.

- Section 5 provides a high-level view of how Software as a Service (SaaS) clouds work.

- Section 6 provides a high-level view of how Platform as a Service (PaaS) clouds work.

- Section 7 provides a high-level view of how Infrastructure as a Service (IaaS) clouds work.

- Section 8 presents open issues.

- Section 9 gives recommendations.

The document also contains appendices with supporting material.

- Appendix A discusses the sharing of responsibilities between providers and consumers for the implementation of security controls.

- Appendix B lists acronyms used in this document.

- Appendix C contains a glossary of terms used in this document.

- Appendix D lists external resources referenced in this document.

- Appendix E lists NIST publications referenced in this document.

2. Cloud Computing Definition

This document uses the NIST Cloud Computing Definition, NIST SP 800-145, to explain characteristics of cloud computing. For the convenience of the reader, the following is excerpted from NIST SP 800-145:

"Cloud computing is a model for enabling convenient, on-demand network access to a shared pool of configurable computing resources (e.g., networks, servers, storage, applications, and services) that can be rapidly provisioned and released with minimal management effort or service provider interaction. This cloud model is composed of five essential characteristics, three service models, and four deployment models.

Essential Characteristics:

On-demand self-service. A consumer can unilaterally provision computing capabilities, such as server time and network storage, as needed automatically without requiring human interaction with each service's provider.

Broad network access. Capabilities are available over the network and accessed through standard mechanisms that promote use by heterogeneous thin or thick client platforms (e.g., mobile phones, tablets, laptops, and workstations).

Resource pooling. The provider's computing resources are pooled to serve multiple consumers using a multi-tenant model, with different physical and virtual resources dynamically assigned and reassigned according to consumer demand. There is a sense of location independence in that the customer generally has no control or knowledge over the exact location of the provided resources but may be able to specify location at a higher level of abstraction (e.g., country, state, or datacenter). Examples of resources include storage, processing, memory, and network bandwidth.

Rapid elasticity. Capabilities can be rapidly and elastically provisioned, in some cases automatically, to scale rapidly outward and inward commensurate with demand. To the consumer, the capabilities available for provisioning often appear to be unlimited and can be appropriated in any quantity at any time.

Measured Service. Cloud systems automatically control and optimize resource use by leveraging a metering capability[1] at some level of abstraction appropriate to the type of service (e.g., storage, processing, bandwidth, and active user accounts). Resource usage can be monitored, controlled, and reported, providing transparency for both the provider and consumer of the utilized service.

Service Models:

Cloud Software as a Service (SaaS). The capability provided to the consumer is to use the provider's applications running on a cloud infrastructure.[2] The applications are accessible from various client devices through a thin client interface such as a Web browser (e.g., Web-based email), or a program interface. The consumer does not manage or control the underlying cloud infrastructure including

---

[1] Typically this is done on a pay-per-use or charge-per-use basis.

[2] A cloud infrastructure is the collection of hardware and software that enables the five essential characteristics of cloud computing. The cloud infrastructure can be viewed as containing both a physical layer and an abstraction layer. The physical layer consists of the hardware resources that are necessary to support the cloud services being provided, and typically includes server, storage and network components. The abstraction layer consists of the software deployed across the physical layer, which manifests the essential cloud characteristics. Conceptually the abstraction layer sits above the physical layer.

network, servers, operating systems, storage, or even individual application capabilities, with the possible exception of limited user-specific application configuration settings.

Cloud Platform as a Service (PaaS). The capability provided to the consumer is to deploy onto the cloud infrastructure consumer-created or -acquired applications created using programming languages and tools supported by the provider.[3] The consumer does not manage or control the underlying cloud infrastructure including network, servers, operating systems, or storage, but has control over the deployed applications and possibly application hosting environment configurations.

Cloud Infrastructure as a Service (IaaS). The capability provided to the consumer is to provision processing, storage, networks, and other fundamental computing resources where the consumer is able to deploy and run arbitrary software, which can include operating systems and applications. The consumer does not manage or control the underlying cloud infrastructure but has control over operating systems, storage, deployed applications; and possibly limited control of select networking components (e.g., host firewalls).

Deployment Models:

Private cloud. The cloud infrastructure is provisioned for exclusive use by a single organization comprising multiple consumers (e.g., business units). It may be owned, managed, and operated by the organization, a third party, or some combination of them, and it may exist on or off premises.

Community cloud. The cloud infrastructure is provisioned for exclusive use by a specific community of consumers from organizations that have shared concerns (e.g., mission, security requirements, policy, and compliance considerations). It may be owned, managed, and operated by one or more of the organizations in the community, a third party, or some combination of them, and it may exist on or off premises.

Public cloud. The cloud infrastructure is provisioned for open use by the general public. It may be owned, managed, and operated by a business, academic, or government organization, or some combination of them. It exists on the premises of the cloud provider.

Hybrid cloud. The cloud infrastructure is a composition of two or more distinct cloud infrastructures (private, community, or public) that remain unique entities, but are bound together by standardized or proprietary technology that enables data and application portability (e.g., cloud bursting for load balancing between clouds)."

Throughout this document, any general use of the term "cloud" or "cloud system" should be assumed to apply to each of the four deployment models. Care is taken to specify a specific deployment model when a statement is not applicable to all four models.

To add clarity, this document uses the following terms consistently:

> **cloud consumer** or **customer**: a person or organization that is a customer of a cloud; note that a cloud customer may itself be a cloud and that clouds may offer services to one another;

> **client**: a machine or software application that accesses a cloud over a network connection, perhaps on behalf of a consumer; and

> **cloud provider** or **provider**: an organization that provides cloud services.

---

[3] This capability does not necessarily preclude the use of compatible programming languages, libraries, services, and tools from other sources.

3. Typical Commercial Terms of Service

A consumer's terms of service for a cloud are determined by a legally binding agreement between the two parties often contained in two parts: (1) a service agreement, and (2) a Service Level Agreement (SLA). Generally, the service agreement is a legal document specifying the rules of the legal contract between a consumer and provider, and the SLA is a shorter document stating the technical performance promises made by a provider including remedies for performance failures. For simplicity, this publication refers to the combination of these two documents as a service agreement.[4]

Service Agreements of various types exist. Service agreements are sometimes used internally between the information systems units and other organizational units of an enterprise to ensure that the information technology services provided are aligned with the mission objectives of the organization. Service agreements are normally not used in agreements for services acquired by one government organization from another. Instead, a Memorandum of Understanding (MOU) or Inter-Agency Agreement (IAA) is typically used to codify the terms of service.

Section 3 discusses certain elements of typical commercial cloud service agreements that directly express the quality of service and security that providers offer. Although the self-service aspect of clouds as defined in the Section 2 implies that a consumer either: (1) accepts a provider's pricing and other terms, or (2) finds a provider with more acceptable terms, potential consumers anticipating heavy use of cloud resources may be able to negotiate more favorable terms. For the typical consumer, however, a cloud's pricing policy and service agreement are nonnegotiable.

Published service agreements between consumers and providers can typically be terminated at any time by either party, either "for cause" such as a consumer's violation of a cloud's acceptable use policies, or for failure of a consumer to pay in a timely manner. Further, an agreement can be terminated for no reason at all. Consumers should analyze provider termination and data retention policies.

Provider promises, including explicit statements regarding limitations, are codified in their service agreements. A provider's service agreement has three basic parts: (1) a collection of promises made to consumers, (2) a collection of promises explicitly not made to consumers, i.e., limitations, and (3) a set of obligations that consumers must accept.

3.1 Promises

Generally, providers make four key promises to consumers:

■ **Availability.** Providers typically advertise availability promises as uptime percentages ranging from 99.5% to 100.0%. These are strong claims, and care is needed to understand how these percentages are calculated. Often, the percentage applies to the number of time intervals within a billing cycle (or longer periods such as a year) in which services are not "up" for the entire interval. Examples of time intervals used by prominent providers are 5 minutes, 15 minutes, and 1 hour. For example, if a provider specifies an availability interval of 15 minutes, and the service is not functional for 14 minutes, 100% availability is preserved using this metric. Generally, the definition of "up" is intuitively defined as service responsiveness, but in some cases, multiple cloud subsystems must fail before the service is judged as unavailable. Providers may also limit availability promises if failures are specific to particular functions or Virtual Machines (VMs).

---

[4] Some cloud providers historically have not provided service agreements, or have provided them only to large or persistent users. An service agreement is extremely important to understand a cloud provider's promises.

- **Remedies for Failure to Perform.** If a provider fails to give the promised availability, a provider should compensate consumers in good faith with a service credit for future use of cloud services. Service credits can be computed in different ways, but are usually determined by how long the service was unavailable within a specific billing period. Service credits are generally capped not to exceed a percentage of a consumer's costs in the billing period in which downtime occurred. Typical caps range from 10% to 100% of a consumer's current costs, depending on the provider. Responsibility for obtaining a service credit is generally placed on the consumer, who must provide timely information about the nature of the outage and the time length of the outage. It is unclear whether a provider will voluntarily inform a consumer of a service disruption. None of the providers recently surveyed (in their standard service agreements) offer a refund or any other remedy for failure to perform; however, all providers should understand that a poor reputation to perform offers few long-term business benefits.

- **Data Preservation.** If a consumer's access to cloud services is terminated "for cause," i.e., because the consumer has violated the clouds' acceptable use policies or for nonpayment, most providers state that they have no obligation to preserve any consumer data remaining in cloud storage. Further, after a consumer voluntarily stops using a cloud, providers generally state that they will not intentionally erase the consumer's data for a period of 30 days. Some providers preserve only a snapshot of consumer data, or recommend that consumers: (1) backup their data outside that provider's cloud inside another provider's cloud, or (2) back it up locally.

- **Legal Care of Consumer Information.** Generally, providers promise not to sell, license, or disclose consumer data except in response to legal requests. Providers, however, usually reserve the right to monitor consumer actions in a cloud, and they may even demand a copy of consumer software to assist in that monitoring.

3.2 Limitations

Generally, provider policies include five key limitations:

- **Scheduled Outages.** If a provider announces a scheduled service outage, the outage does not count as failure to perform. For some providers, outages must be announced in advance, or must be bounded in duration.

- **Force majeure events.** Providers generally disclaim responsibility for events outside their realistic control. Examples include power failures, natural disasters, and failures in network connectivity between consumers and providers.

- **Service Agreement Changes.** Providers generally reserve the right to change the terms of the service agreement at any time, and to change pricing with limited advanced notice. For standard service agreement changes, notice is generally given by a provider by posting the change to a Web site. It is then the consumer's responsibility to periodically check the Web site for changes. Changes may take effect immediately or after a delay of several weeks. For changes that affect an individual consumer's account, notice may be delivered via email or a delivery service.

- **Security.** Providers generally assert that they are not responsible for the impacts of security breaches or for security in general, i.e., unauthorized modification or disclosure of consumer data, or service interruptions caused by malicious activity. Generally, service agreements are explicit about placing security risks on consumers. In some cases, providers promise to use best efforts to protect consumer data, but all of the providers surveyed disclaim security responsibility for data breach, data loss, or service interruptions by limiting remedies to service credits for failure to meet availability promises. Further, it is unclear how easy it would be for a consumer to determine that a service disruption was maliciously induced versus induction from another source.

■ **Service API Changes.** Providers generally reserve the right to change or delete service Application Programming Interfaces (APIs) at any time.

3.3 Obligations

Generally, consumers must agree to three key obligations:

■ **Acceptable Use Polices.** Consumers generally must agree to refrain from storing illegal content, such as child pornography, and from conducting illegal activities such as: (1) gambling, (2) sending spam, (3) conducting security attacks (e.g., denial of service or hacking), (4) distributing spyware, (5) intrusive monitoring, and (6) attempting to subvert cloud system infrastructures. Acceptable use policies vary among providers.

■ **Licensed Software.** All providers state that third-party software running in their clouds must conform to the software's license terms. In some cases, providers bundle such software and include monitoring to ensure that license restrictions are enforced.

■ **Timely Payments.** Cloud service costs are generally incurred gradually over a billing period, with the fee due to the provider at the period's end. Failure to pay, after a grace period, usually subjects a consumer to suspension or termination "for cause" which can result in loss of consumer data.

3.4 Recommendations

■ **Terminology.** Consumers should pay close attention to the terms that are used in service agreements. Common terms may be redefined by a cloud provider in ways that are specific to that provider's offerings.

■ **Remedies.** Unless a specific service agreement has been negotiated with a provider, remedies for any failures are likely to be extremely limited; consumers may wish to formulate and negotiate remedies that are commensurate with damage that might be sustained.

■ **Compliance.** Consumers should carefully assess whether the service agreement specifies compliance with appropriate laws and regulations governing consumer data.

■ **Security, Criticality, and Backup.** Consumers should carefully examine the service agreement for any disclaimers relating to security or critical processing, and should also search for any comment on whether the provider recommends independent backup of data stored in their cloud.

■ **Negotiated Service Agreement.** If the terms of the default service agreement do not address all consumer needs, the consumer should discuss modifications of the service agreement with the provider prior to use.

■ **Service Agreement Changes.** Be aware that, depending on the details of the service agreement, a provider may change the terms of service with a specified level of advance notice. Changes may affect both price and quality of service. It is prudent to develop a plan to migrate workloads to alternate cloud providers, or back on-premise, in the event that a change in service terms is unacceptable.

4.   General Cloud Environments

At the time of this writing, many individuals and organizations have made general statements about cloud computing, its advantages, and its weaknesses. It is important to understand, however, that the term "cloud computing" encompasses a variety of systems and technologies as well as service and deployment models, and business models. A number of claims that are sometimes made about cloud computing, e.g., that it "scales," or that it converts capital expenses to operational expenses, are only true for some kinds of cloud systems. The goal of this section is to clearly describe a division of cloud computing systems into five significant scenarios and, for each scenario, to explain general issues about cloud computing, such as scalability, and how those issues apply in that scenario.[5]

As implied by the NIST cloud computing definition, a cloud system is a collection of network-accessible computing resources that customers (i.e., cloud consumers) can access over a network. In general terms, a cloud system and its consumers employ the client-server model [Com88], which means that consumers (the clients) send messages over a network to server computers, which then perform work in response to the messages received.

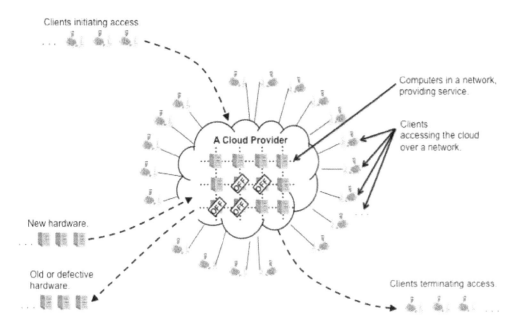

Figure 1: General Cloud and Consumer View

Figure 1 gives a general view of a cloud and its clients: the cloud's computing resources are depicted as a grid of computer systems where clients access a cloud over network connections. As shown in the figure, new clients may arrive, existing clients may depart, and the number of clients using a cloud at any one time is variable. Similarly, a cloud maintains a pool of hardware resources that it manages to maximize service and minimize costs. To maintain highly available services despite expected component failures and service life expirations, a cloud incorporates new hardware components as needed and retires old or failing components. To provide services cost-effectively, a cloud will manage the pool of hardware resources for resource efficiency; one of the strategies that a cloud provider employs during periods of reduced consumer demand is to power off unused components. Whether for power management, or for

_____

[5] This section presents a physical, network-oriented view of how cloud systems can be connected with consumers. An understanding of cloud software and of which parts of the traditional software "stack" are made available to consumers is also important, and is presented in Sections 5, 6, and 7.

hardware refresh, migration of customer workloads (data storage and processing) from one physical computer to another physical computer [Chr05, Shr10, VMw11, Mic10, Red99] is a key strategy that allows a provider to refresh hardware or consolidate workloads without inconveniencing consumers.

From Figure 1, a small number of general statements about cloud computing (e.g., strengths and limitations, performance characteristics) can be inferred; organizations considering the use of cloud computing should consider these general statements (listed below). Many statements commonly made about clouds (e.g., that clouds scale for very large workloads or that clouds replace capital expenses with operational expenses), however, are true only for certain types of clouds. To avoid confusion, this document explicitly qualifies each such statement with the type of cloud to which it applies; i.e., each statement has a "scope." The scopes used in this document are listed in Table 1.

Table 1: Scope Modifiers for Statements Asserted About Clouds

Scope Name	Applicability
general	Applies to all cloud deployment models.
on-site-private	Applies to private clouds implemented at a customer's premises.
outsourced-private	Applies to private clouds where the server side is outsourced to a hosting company.
on-site-community	Applies to community clouds implemented on the premises of the customers composing a community cloud.
outsourced-community	Applies to community clouds where the server side is outsourced to a hosting company.
public	Applies to public clouds.

Each of the scopes is explained below. The following statements are general in their scope, i.e., they apply regardless of the deployment model or service model:

- **Network dependency (general).** The consumers, being clients, need a working and secure network to access a cloud. If the network is not reliable, the cloud will not be reliable from the consumer's point of view.

- **Consumers still need IT skills (general).** By operating the server computers, a provider may reduce the need for IT staff in consumer organizations, but consumers will still access the cloud from on-site consumer-managed client systems that must be maintained, secure, etc.

- **Workload locations are dynamically assigned and are thus hidden from clients (general).** To manage a cloud's hardware resources efficiently, providers must be able to migrate consumer workloads between machines without inconveniencing the clients, i.e., without the clients being required to track and adapt to changes and therefore without the clients being aware.[6]

- **Risks from multi-tenancy (general).** The workloads of different clients may reside concurrently on the same system and local network, separated only by access policies implemented by a provider's software. A flaw in the implementation or in the provider's management and operational policies and procedures could compromise the security of consumers.

---

[6] In some cases (e.g., the IaaS service model described in Section 7 below) a workload may exist in a particular location for a specific time before it migrates; in other cases (e.g., for the PaaS service model described in Section 6 below) a workload may exist as a fundamentally distributed entity with sequential operations performed for a consumer potentially executing in different servers, and data existing in a geographically distributed data store.

■ **Data import/export, and performance limitations (general).** Because consumers access a cloud over a network, on-demand bulk data import or export may exceed the network's ability to carry the data in a timely manner. Additionally, real-time or critical processing may be problematic because of networking latency or other limitations.

Organizations contemplating the use of cloud computing should consider these general statements and their possible consequences for an organization's mission and business model. Considering only the general statements, however, is not sufficient. Clouds are also described by one or more of the other (i.e., not "general") scopes listed in Table 1; organizations contemplating the use of cloud computing should consider the detailed statements made for the kinds of clouds they contemplate using. Each of the alternatives is broken out below in a separate section focusing on a specific scope.[7]

4.1 Understanding Who Controls Resources in a Cloud

It is sometimes asserted that when compared to traditional on premises computing, cloud computing requires consumers to give up (to providers) two important capabilities:

■ **Control:** the ability to decide, with high confidence, who and what is allowed to access consumer data and programs, and the ability to perform actions (such as erasing data or disconnecting a network) with high confidence both that the actions have been taken and that no additional actions were taken that would subvert the consumer's intent (e.g., a consumer request to erase a data object should not be subverted by the silent generation of a copy).

■ **Visibility:** the ability to monitor, with high confidence, the status of a consumer's data and programs and how consumer data and programs are being accessed by others.

The extent, however, to which consumers may need to relinquish control or visibility depends on a number of factors including physical possession and the ability to configure (with high confidence) protective access boundary mechanisms around a consumer's computing resources.

This document uses the concept of access boundaries to organize and characterize the different cloud deployment models. Figure 2 illustrates a key concept from computer security relating to boundaries and control, the security perimeter [TIS94, Gas88]. As shown in the figure, a security perimeter is a barrier to access: entities that are inside the perimeter may freely access resources inside the perimeter; however entities that are located outside the perimeter may access the resources inside only if allowed by a boundary controller that enforces a policy over access. Although the term is often used to discuss firewalls and networks, the concept of the security perimeter is actually more generic and can be used, for instance, to describe the boundaries between different privilege levels of running software, e.g., between applications and operating systems. By itself, a security perimeter is NOT an adequate security mechanism; however, perimeter controls are an important building block for secure systems.

Typical boundary controllers include firewalls [TIS94, Che94], guards [Eps99], and Virtual Private Networks [Ros99]. By implementing a security perimeter around its important resources, an organization can achieve both a measure of control over the use of those resources and a means for monitoring access to them.[8] Furthermore, via reconfiguration, an organization can adapt a security perimeter to changing needs (e.g., blocking or allowing protocols or data formats based on changing business circumstances).

---

[7] This document does not generally repeat text. However, for specific types of clouds, more can be said about them; in this case, the name of a general statement may be used again but with an explanation specific to that type of cloud.

[8] When uncontrolled paths to computing resources exist, a security perimeter is weakened or may not even exist. Pervasive wireless communications, e.g., are a threat to security perimeters since there may be no reliable way to interpose a boundary controller between external entities and internal entities. Similarly, many organizations use mobile devices that are sometimes connected within an organization's security perimeter, and sometimes exposed directly, e.g., when on travel.

The various cloud deployment models in the NIST cloud definition have implications for the locations of consumer-controlled security perimeters and hence for the level of control that consumers can exercise over resources that they entrust to a cloud.

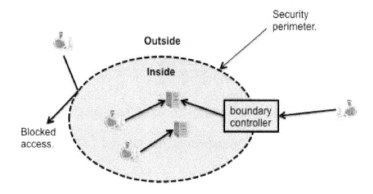

Figure 2: The Security Perimeter

The NIST cloud definition lists four deployment models: private, community, public, and hybrid. The private and community deployment models, however, admit of two variants that should be discussed separately because they affect the security perimeter: on-site, and outsourced. The hybrid deployment model is a combination of the others and therefore a hybrid deployment may be subject to the implications of all of its building blocks as well as unique implications that arise when multiple systems are composed into more complex integrated systems.

4.2   The On-site Private Cloud Scenario

Figure 3 presents a simple view of an on-site private cloud. As shown in the figure, the security perimeter extends around both the consumer's on-site resources and the private cloud's resources. The private cloud may be centralized at a single consumer site or may be distributed over several consumer sites. The security perimeter will exist only if the consumer implements it. If implemented, the security perimeter will not guarantee control over the private cloud's resources, but its existence gives an opportunity for a consumer to exercise control over resources entrusted to the on-site private cloud.

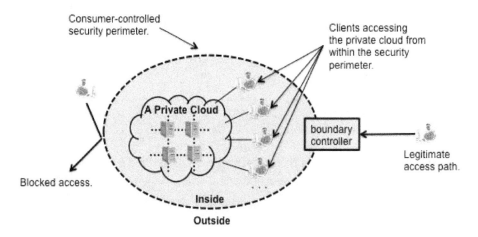

Figure 3: On-site Private Cloud

Although the general implications remain true with an on-site private cloud, the on-site-private scenario allows for additional and more detailed implications that organizations considering the use of an on-site private cloud should consider:

■ **Network dependency (on-site-private).** Depending on the configuration (e.g., single physical site, protected cloud network), the network dependency for an on-site private cloud may be limited to dependence on networking resources over which a consumer has control (e.g., local area networking). In this scenario, larger-scale network problems, such as Internet congestion or communications with remote Internet Domain Name Servers (DNS) [Moc87-1, Moc87-2] may be avoided.

If a consumer organization spans multiple physical sites and wishes different sites to access the same private cloud, however, the consumer must either provision a controlled inter-site communications media, such as an encrypted leased line, or must use cryptography (e.g., with a VPN) over less controlled communications media such as the public Internet. Both of these options introduce risks to a private cloud's networking availability and security because performance dependencies are established to resources that exist off of the consumer's site and that are not directly under the consumer's control, and because any failure to implement and configure cryptographic mechanisms could allow outsiders access. The consumer organization must also ensure that remote sites are maintained at an appropriate security level for the private cloud or that boundary devices are installed to prevent inconsistencies in security levels.

■ **Consumers still need IT skills (on-site-private).** Consumer organizations will need the traditional IT skills required to manage user devices that access the private cloud, and will require cloud IT skills as well. Early in the rollout of an on-site private cloud, consumer organizations may wish to maintain parallel cloud and non-cloud operations for an evaluation period. During any such evaluation period, traditional IT skills will be required. Even after an evaluation period, however, traditional IT staff will be needed (perhaps at reduced levels) to manage legacy licensing agreements, special hardware or system requirements, unique security needs for special projects, and legacy investments in equipment and training.

In addition, new skills for working in clouds may be required. For example, an organization that performs compute-intensive jobs may need to eventually reorganize those jobs so that they can run using a higher level of parallelism on the cloud's resources [Dea04]; an organization that processes large data sets in the cloud will need to develop skills with cloud-based storage [Cha06, Ghe03, Ama06, SNI10, Msf11].[9]

■ **Workload locations are hidden from clients (on-site-private).** As in the general case, to manage a cloud's hardware resources, a private cloud must be able to migrate workloads between machines without inconveniencing clients, i.e., without the clients being aware. In some situations, to avoid creating a single point of failure, it may also be necessary to provision and operate redundant cloud facilities at geographically diverse locations. With an on-site private cloud, however, a consumer organization chooses the physical infrastructure in which the private cloud operates, and hence determines the possible geographical locations of workloads. While individual clients still may not know where their workloads physically exist within the consumer organization's infrastructure at any given time, the consumer organization has both visibility and control over where workloads are allowed to reside.

■ **Risks from multi-tenancy (on-site-private).** As in the general case, the workloads of different clients may reside concurrently on the same systems and local networks, separated only by access policies implemented by a cloud provider's software. A flaw in the implementation or in the

---

[9] Note: this is not a comprehensive list of cloud storage systems.

provider's management and operational policies and procedures could compromise the security of a consumer organization by exposing client workloads to one another contrary to the consumer's security policy. Logical segregation techniques at the network layer, such as VPN Routing and Forwarding (VRF), can help mitigate risks. An on-site private cloud mitigates these risks somewhat further by restricting the number of possible attackers; all of the clients would typically be members of the consumer organization or authorized guests or partners, but the on-site private cloud is still vulnerable to attack conducted by authorized but also malicious insiders. Different organizational functions, such as payroll, storage of sensitive personally identifiable information, or the generation of intellectual property may be merged as a consequence of such security failures, which can provide access to users who are not authorized to access specific classes of data and who then may disclose data from the on-site private cloud.

■ **Data import/export, and performance limitations (on-site-private).** As with the general case, on-demand bulk data import/export is limited by the on-site private cloud's network capacity, and real-time or critical processing may be problematic because of networking limitations. In the on-site private cloud scenario, however, these limits may be adjusted, although not eliminated, by provisioning high-performance and/or high-reliability networking within the consumer's infrastructure. Particularly if a consumer has only one site that requires access to the on-site private cloud, a consumer may be able to provision local networks that provide higher performance than can practically be achieved via wide area networks.

■ **Potentially strong security from external threats (on-site-private).** In an on-site private cloud, a consumer has the option of implementing an appropriately strong security perimeter to protect private cloud resources against external threats to the same level of security as can be achieved for non-cloud resources. For low-impact data and processing, the security perimeter may consist of commercial firewall rule sets and VPNs. For higher-impact data, security perimeters can be constructed via more restrictive firewall policies [Zwi00, Ran99], multi-factor authentication [SP-800-63], encryption [Sch94, Ros99], intrusion detection and prevention, and even physical isolation.

■ **Significant-to-high up-front costs to migrate into the cloud (on-site-private).** An on-site private cloud requires that cloud management software be installed on computer systems within a consumer organization. If the cloud is intended to support process-intensive or data-intensive workloads, the software will need to be installed on numerous commodity systems or on a more limited number of high-performance systems. Installing cloud software and managing the installations will incur significant up-front costs, even if the cloud software itself is free, and even if much of the hardware already exists within a consumer organization. Three potential approaches to accomplish this are:

New Data Center: The most direct approach is for a consumer to provision a data center in which to deploy the cloud software. In this case, the on-site private cloud incurs up-front costs that are similar to those of a typical data center and the consumer can provision the data center for anticipated workloads.

Converted Data Center: As an alternative to provisioning a new data center, a consumer may convert part or all of an existing data center to support the on-site private cloud. This approach, however, may not be compatible with running parallel cloud and non-cloud systems during the initial evaluation period.

Scavenged Resources: Another alternative approach, supported by [Nur-08, Nur-08-2], is for cloud software to be installed primarily on computers that already exist within an organization. In this scenario, cloud systems share hardware resources with other uses of the hardware and essentially can harvest cycles that might otherwise be wasted. This approach offers the advantage that cloud services can be made available on an experimental basis without a large hardware investment; however, the resources available to such a configuration will be limited to the previously-surplus resources in the organization's infrastructure (unless the former uses of the hardware are reduced in favor of the cloud). Additional limitations are that: (1) hardware resources must be incorporated into the on-site private cloud from wherever they exist in a consumer organization's infrastructure (via networking) rather than being co-located for efficiency, and (2) the available hardware may not be homogeneous and thus may be somewhat more difficult to administer.

- **Limited resources (on-site-private).** An on-site private cloud, at any specific time, has a fixed computing and storage capacity that has been sized to correspond to anticipated workloads and cost restrictions. If an organization is large enough and supports a sufficient diversity of workloads, an on-site private cloud may be able to provide elasticity to clients within the consumer organization. Smaller on-site private clouds will, however, exhibit maximum capacity limits similar to those of traditional data centers. An on-site private cloud also requires that some costs, e.g., for equipment, be paid up-front.

4.3 The Outsourced Private Cloud Scenario

Figure 4 depicts an outsourced private cloud. As shown in the figure, an outsourced private cloud has two security perimeters, one implemented by a cloud consumer (on the right) and one implemented by a provider[10] (left). The two security perimeters are joined by a protected communications link. As is apparent from the figure, the security of data and processing conducted in the outsourced private cloud depends on the strength and availability of both security perimeters and of the protected communication link. The provider thus accepts a responsibility to enforce the provider-implemented security perimeter and to prevent mingling of private cloud resources with other cloud resources that are outside the provider-controlled security perimeter. The suitability of various mechanisms for achieving an appropriate strength of separation between private cloud resources and other cloud resources depends on the consumer's security requirements. A number of possible mechanisms could be used with various tradeoffs between separation strength and cost/convenience (e.g., Virtual Local Area Network (VLAN), VPN, separate network segments or clusters). This scenario, however, should, not merely employ separation mechanisms that are identical to the normal mechanisms (e.g., hardware virtualization, VLANs) that separate customers in a public cloud. If those mechanisms alone were used, this scenario would essentially become the public cloud scenario.

---

[10] But perhaps configured by the consumer.

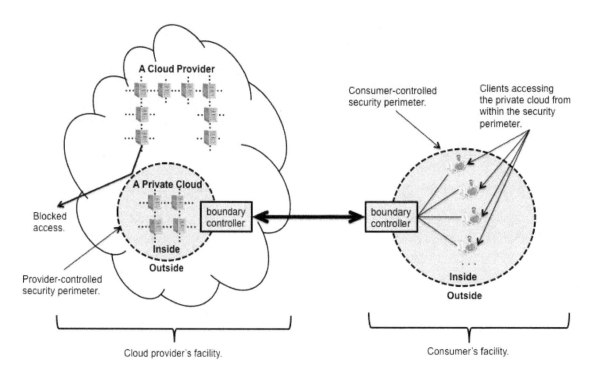

Figure 4: Outsourced Private Cloud

Although the general statements remain true for the outsourced private scenario, the outsourced private scenario also allows for a more detailed understanding of some of the general statements plus additional statements that organizations considering the use of an outsourced private cloud should consider:

■ **Network Dependency (outsourced-private).** In the outsourced private scenario, consumers may have an option to provision dedicated protected and reliable communication links with the provider. Although network dependence does not appear to be avoidable, in this scenario the impact of the network dependency may be ameliorated at a negotiated price (e.g., dedicated leased network connections supporting enhanced performance, reliability, and security).

■ **Workload locations are hidden from clients (outsourced-private).** As in the general case, to manage a cloud's hardware resources, an outsourced private cloud must be able to migrate workloads between machines without inconveniencing the clients, i.e., without the clients being aware of the migrations. The outsourced private cloud scenario, however, provides an opportunity for the consumer's organization to have some visibility and control regarding workload locations. Assuming that the provider faithfully implements the security perimeter agreed upon with the consumer, the consumer organization workloads move only within the agreed-upon security perimeter. Depending on the mechanisms chosen to implement the perimeter, the consumer may know the physical location (e.g., cluster, network segments) of the resources devoted to the outsourced private cloud even though the clients are unaware.

■ **Risks from multi-tenancy (outsourced-private).** The implications are the same as those for an on-site private cloud. FISMA and OMB policy require that external cloud providers handling federal information or operating information systems on behalf of the federal government meet the same security requirements as federal agencies.

■ **Data import/export, and performance limitations (outsourced-private).** As with the general case, on-demand bulk data import/export is limited by the network capacity between a provider and consumer, and real-time or critical processing may be problematic because of networking limitations.

In the outsourced private cloud scenario, however, these limits may be adjusted, although not eliminated, by provisioning high-performance and/or high-reliability networking between the provider and consumer. This provisioning, however, would require a special contract and incur significant costs.

■ **Potentially strong security from external threats (outsourced-private).** As with the on-site private cloud scenario, a variety of techniques exist to harden a security perimeter. The main difference with the outsourced private cloud is that the techniques need to be applied both to a consumer's perimeter and to a provider's perimeter, and that the communications link needs to be protected.

■ **Modest-to-significant up-front costs to migrate into the cloud (outsourced-private).** Unlike the case of an on-site private cloud, where physical computing resources need to be provisioned or scavenged by a consumer before the cloud can start operating, in the outsourced private cloud scenario, the resources are provisioned by the provider, and the main startup costs for the consumer relate to: (1) negotiating the terms of the service level agreement (e.g., agreeing on suitable protection mechanisms), (2) possibly upgrading the consumer's network to connect to the outsourced private cloud, (3) switching from traditional applications to cloud-hosted applications, (4) porting existing non-cloud operations to the cloud, and (5) training. Although these costs may be significant, they do not include server-side equipment and its supporting infrastructure.

■ **Extensive resources available (outsourced-private).** Unlike the case of an on-site private cloud, in which the resources must be provisioned by a consumer up front, in the case of the outsourced private cloud, a consumer can rent resources in any quantity offered by the provider. Provisioning and operating computing equipment at scale is a core competency of providers. Hence it is likely that a provider can provision relatively large private clouds as needed. As with the on-site private cloud, an outsourced private cloud has a fixed capacity at any given time, and providing elasticity for clients is achievable only if the cloud is large enough and there is sufficient diversity of workloads. As with an on-site private cloud, an outsourced private cloud will exhibit maximum capacity limits similar to those of traditional data centers.

4.4 The On-site Community Cloud Scenario

Figure 5 depicts an on-site community cloud. The community depicted in the figure is made up of a set of participant organizations. Each participant organization may provide cloud services, consume cloud services, or both. It is necessary for at least one community member to provide cloud services for a community cloud to be functional. The figure depicts members that provide cloud services (and possibly consume them also) on the left and those that consume-only on the right. Assuming that each organization implements a security perimeter, the participant organizations are connected via links between the boundary controllers that allow access through their security perimeters. Optionally, organizations may implement extra security perimeters to isolate the local cloud resources from other local resources. Many network configurations are possible; the figure shows the extra security perimeter as being inside an organization's "non-cloud" security perimeter although it could be located outside as well. The boundary controllers in any configuration should grant appropriate access to the cloud resources both to local clients and to clients of other participant organizations. Importantly, providing access to local cloud resources should not grant access to non-cloud resources unless granting such access is a specific policy goal.

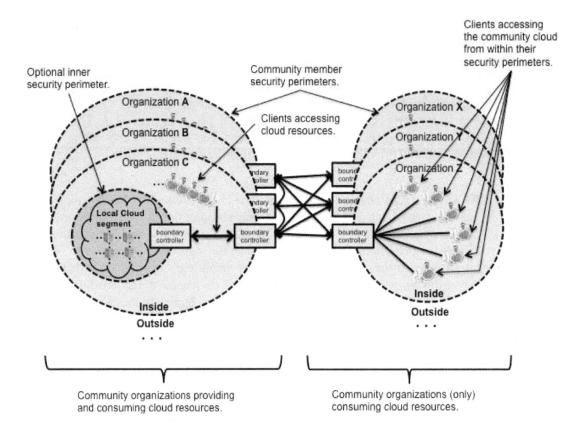

Figure 5: On-site Community Cloud

In Figure 5 it is easy to see that the access policy of a community cloud may be complex: if there are N community members, a decision must be made, either implicitly or explicitly, on how to share a member's local cloud resources with each of the other members. A number of policy specification techniques (e.g., discretionary access control using a standard such as XACML [Mos05], or following a security model such as role-based access control [Fer92] or attribute-based access control [Kar09]) might be used to express sharing policies. Besides controlling access to resources, identity management [Oid11, Rag08, Oix10] is important in this scenario since clients from multiple participant organizations access a common pool of resources.

As with the on-site private cloud and the outsourced private cloud, although the general statements remain true for the on-site community scenario, the on-site community cloud scenario also allows for a more detailed understanding of some of the general statements as well as additional statements that organizations considering the use of an on-site community cloud should consider:

■ **Network Dependency (on-site community).** As with the on-site private scenario, where the organization spans multiple sites, the consumers in an on-site community cloud need to either provision controlled inter-site communication links or use cryptography over a less controlled communications media (such as the public Internet). The reliability and security of the community cloud will depend on the reliability and security of the communication links. Dedicated leased network connections can also be used to support enhanced performance, reliability, and security. In the on-site community case, in addition, care should be taken to understand the actual dependencies between member organizations since there are multiple organizations participating and any subset of them could suffer a cloud infrastructure failure (e.g., going offline). Additionally, local clouds will probably need to be taken offline for maintenance at various times and therefore two-way communication in advance among the community members is essential to achieving a clear understanding of the service levels that they offer to one another and require from one another.

- **Consumers still need IT skills (on-site-community).** In an on-site community cloud, there are potentially two classes of participant organizations: those who provide cloud services to the community, and those who only consume cloud resources. For the participant organizations that provide cloud resources, the IT skills required are similar to those required for the on-site private cloud scenario except that the overall cloud configuration may be more complex and hence require a higher skill level. If any participant organizations are consumers only, the IT skills required are similar to those of the general case except that if there are multiple participant organizations providing cloud services, the configuration from the consuming side may be more complex, e.g., forcing clients to maintain multiple authentication credentials or to commit to an identity management framework.

  Identity and access control configurations among the participant organizations may be complex; organizations considering a community cloud should ensure that the IT staff from the participant organizations negotiate and clearly document the access policies that are planned within the community cloud.

- **Workload locations are hidden from clients (on-site-community).** As with the outsourced private cloud scenario, assuming that participant organizations faithfully implement their security perimeters and have policies to keep workloads onsite, workloads should remain within participant organizations. Variations on this scenario are possible, however. For example, a participant organization providing cloud services to the community cloud may wish to employ an outsourced private cloud as a part of its implementation strategy. An organization that is concerned with knowing workload locations should discuss potential outsourcing configurations prior to joining a community cloud, and should ensure that the outsourcing policies are clearly documented for the participant organizations.

- **Risks from multi-tenancy (on-site-community).** As with the on-site private scenario, the on-site community scenario mitigates some of the multi-tenancy risks by restricting the number of possible attackers. In the on-site community scenario, however, the cloud encompasses more organizations and hence may restrict the set of potential attackers less than in the case of the on-site private scenario.

- **Data import/export, and performance limitations (on-site-community).** The communication links between the various participant organizations in a community cloud can be provisioned to various levels of performance, security and reliability, based on the needs of the participant organizations. The network-based limitations are thus similar to those of the outsourced-private cloud scenario.

- **Potentially strong security from external threats (on-site-community).** The security of a community cloud from external threats depends on the security of all the security perimeters of the participant organizations and the strength of the communications links. These dependencies are essentially similar to those of the outsourced private cloud scenario, but with possibly more links and security perimeters and greater configuration complexity.

- **Highly variable up-front costs to migrate into the cloud (on-site-community).** The up-front costs of an on-site community cloud for a participant organization depend greatly on whether the organization plans to consume cloud services only or also to provide cloud services. For the consume-only scenario, the up-front costs appear to be similar to those for an outsourced private cloud (i.e., modest-to-significant). For a participant organization that intends to provide cloud services within the community cloud, the costs appear to be similar to those for the on-site private cloud scenario (i.e., significant-to-high).

- **Limited resources (on-site community).** As with the on-site private cloud scenario, resources for an on-site community cloud must be provisioned or scavenged locally. Therefore the resource limitations appear to be similar to those of the on-site private cloud, i.e., relatively limited.

4.5   The Outsourced Community Cloud Scenario

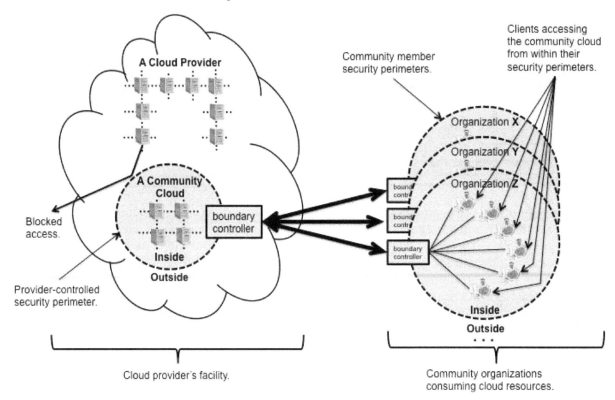

Figure 6: Outsourced Community Cloud

Figure 6 depicts an outsourced community cloud. The community depicted in the figure is made up of a set of participant organizations that consume cloud services. This scenario is very similar to the outsourced private cloud scenario: server-side responsibilities are managed by a cloud provider that implements a security perimeter and that prevents mingling of community cloud resources with other cloud resources that are outside the provider-controlled security perimeter. A significant difference is that the cloud provider may need to enforce a sharing policy among participant organizations in the community cloud.

Although the general statements remain true for the outsourced community cloud scenario, the outsourced community cloud scenario also allows for a more detailed view of some of the general statements as follows:

- **Network dependency (outsourced-community).** As can be seen from Figure 6, the network dependency of the outsourced community cloud is similar to that of the outsourced private cloud. The primary difference is that multiple protected communications links are likely from the community members to the provider's facility.

- **Workload locations are hidden from clients (outsourced-community).** The implications appear to be the same as for the outsourced private cloud scenario.

- **Risks from multi-tenancy (outsourced-community).** The implications appear to be the same as for the on-site community cloud scenario.

- **Data import/export, and performance limitations (outsourced-community).** The implications appear to be the same as for the outsourced private cloud scenario.

- **Potentially strong security from external threats (outsourced-community).** The implications appear to be the similar to those for the on-site community cloud scenario.

- **Modest-to-significant up-front costs to migrate into the cloud (outsourced-community).** The implications appear to be the same as for the outsourced private cloud scenario.

- **Extensive resources available (outsourced-community).** The implications appear to be the same as for the outsourced private cloud scenario.

4.6   The Public Cloud Scenario

Figure 7 depicts a public cloud. This diagram is essentially similar to Figure 1 except that a consumer facility implementing a security perimeter is shown. In the case of a public cloud, however, more statements can be made based on the diagram than could be made based on Figure 1. For example, in the public setting, the provider's computing and storage resources are potentially large; the communication links can be assumed to be implemented over the public Internet; and the cloud serves a diverse pool of clients (and possibly attackers).

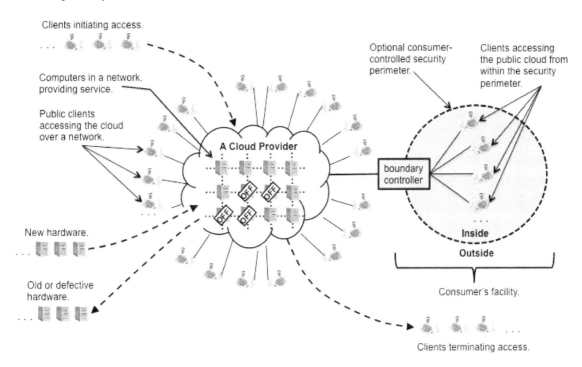

Figure 7: Public Cloud

As with the other scenarios, although the general statements remain true for the public cloud scenario, the public cloud scenario also allows for a more detailed view of some of the general statements:

■ **Network dependency (public).** In the public scenario, consumers connect to providers via the public Internet. The dependability of connections thus depends on the Internet's infrastructure of Domain Name System (DNS) servers, the router infrastructure, and the inter-router links. The reliability of connections can thus be affected by misconfiguration [Opp03] or failure of these components as well as network congestion or attack. Additionally, consumers require a connection via an Internet Service Provider, often designated the "last mile." This connection must also be functional for the cloud to be accessible.

■ **Workload locations are hidden from clients (public).** In the public scenario, a provider may migrate a consumer's workload, whether processing or data, at any time. One of the central arguments for cost efficiency in public cloud computing is that data centers (and hence workloads) can be located where costs are low. Generally, workloads in a public cloud may be relocated anywhere at any time unless the provider has offered (optional) location restriction policies and the consumer has configured their account to request specific location restrictions. Generally, location restrictions in a public cloud are somewhat coarse grained (e.g., the east coast of the US). The confidence that restrictions are actually enforced rests upon protection of consumer credentials (e.g., that the account has not been hijacked and had its location preferences changed) and the faithfulness with which the provider implements the advertised policies. Generally, consumers are not in a position to verify that location restrictions have been enforced.

■ **Risks from multi-tenancy (public).** In a public cloud, a single machine may be shared by the workloads of any combination of consumers. In practice, this means that a consumer's workload may be co-resident with the workloads of competitors or adversaries. As summarized in the general case, this introduces both reliability and security risk. A failure could occur or an attack could be perpetrated by any consumer. Scaling to larger sets of consumers and resources is one of the important strategies for public clouds to achieve low costs and elasticity; if this scaling is achieved, however, it also implies a large collection of potential attackers.

■ **Limited visibility and control over data regarding security (public).** The details of provider system operation are usually considered proprietary information and are not divulged to consumers. In many cases, the software employed by a provider is proprietary and likely not available for examination by consumers. Consequently, consumers do not (at the time of this writing) have a guaranteed way to monitor or authorize access to their resources in the cloud. Although providers may make strong efforts to carry out the requests of consumers and some may provide monitoring services, consumers must either trust that the provider is performing operations with fidelity or, if the provider has contracted with a third party auditing organization, trust that the auditing is accurate and timely. As an example of this limitation, a consumer cannot currently verify that data has been completely deleted from a provider's systems.

■ **Low up-front costs to migrate into the cloud (public).** The implications appear to be the same as for the outsourced private cloud scenario.

■ **Elasticity: illusion of unlimited resource availability (public).** Public clouds are generally unrestricted in their location or size. Additionally, they can generally use multi-tenancy without being limited by static security perimeters, which allows a potentially high degree of flexibility in the movement of consumer workloads to correspond with available resources. As a consequence, public clouds have unique advantages in achieving elasticity, or the illusion (to consumers) of unlimited resource availability.

■ **Restrictive default service level agreements (public).** The default service level agreements of public clouds specify limited promises that providers make to subscribers, limit the remedies available to subscribers, and outline subscriber obligations in obtaining such remedies.

■ Although marketing literature may make broad claims about cloud system reliability, security, etc., the terms of the service agreements define the actual (legal) obligations of providers. Section 3 describes these terms in greater detail.

4.7 The Hybrid Cloud Scenario

As given by the cloud definition in Section 2, a hybrid cloud is composed of two or more private, community, or public clouds. As presented in this section, both the private and the community deployment models have two significant variations: on-site and outsourced. The variations are significant because they have different performance, reliability, and security properties, among others. A hybrid cloud, consequently, is a composition of clouds where each constituent cloud is one of the five variants. There are many conceivable configurations of hybrid clouds and it is not realistic to enumerate them. However, the space of possibilities and the potential challenges can be illustrated.

Figure 8 depicts a theoretical hybrid cloud composed of a number of constituent clouds representing all of the deployment model variants. The figure depicts access points into the constituent clouds as well as the network connectivity between them. Security policies governing the flow of information and access to resources could be implemented in a wide variety of ways, e.g., based on policies applied by each individual constituent cloud. Additionally, global issues such as identity management and shared standards for authentication and information protection within the hybrid cloud are not shown. A further complication not shown is that a hybrid cloud may change over time with constituent clouds joining and leaving.

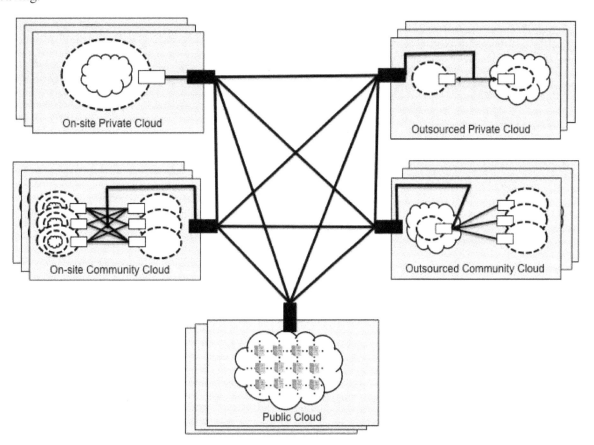

Figure 8: Hybrid Cloud

As depicted in Figure 8, a hybrid cloud can be extremely complex. However many less complex and highly useful hybrid cloud configurations are possible. For example, "cloud bursting" is an often-discussed concept in which a consumer uses a private cloud for routine workloads, but optionally accesses one or more external clouds during periods of high demand. Using one type of cloud to provide backup resources to another [SNI09] is another hybrid possibility as well as using one cloud for disaster recovery [SNI09] for a second. For new software developed specifically to run on cloud platforms (e.g., [Msf11-2, Goo11, Sal11]), multi-cloud configurations are possible and even likely. For example, Web request handling platform clouds (see Section 6) can be very efficient for making Web applications continuously available at low cost while on-site or community infrastructure clouds may be more suitable for performing necessary background work to support the applications. Different cloud deployment variants may also be appropriate for particular organizational functions or roles; for example, an organization may elect to process sensitive data such as payroll information in an outsourced private cloud but use a public cloud for new software development and testing activities.

5. Software-as-a-Service Environments

The purpose of this section is to describe the architecture and basic operation of SaaS, or Software as a Service, in a cloud-computing environment. This information is important for readers who need to evaluate whether a SaaS cloud offering can satisfy particular reliability, compliance, or security requirements, and also for readers who want to understand operational mechanisms.

The term SaaS dates from the 1990s and thus predates the term cloud computing. SaaS is also known commonly as "Web services." SaaS systems can be implemented in a number of different ways; using the SaaS maturity model of [Cho06], the most advanced architectures for SaaS appear to satisfy the NIST definition of cloud computing. While many slightly different definitions of SaaS are possible, a simple and usable definition has already been formulated:

"Software deployed as a hosted service and accessed over the Internet." [Cho06]

Fundamentally, cloud computing provides convenient rental of computing resources. These resources, which are typically accessed by consumers over a network, must be measurable in units that can be

SaaS

Who are the consumers?
1. Organizations providing their members or employees with access to typical software applications such as office productivity or email.
2. End users who directly use software applications, whether on their own behalf or that of their organization.
3. Software application administrators who configure an application for end users.

What does a consumer get? The right to use specific applications on demand, and application data management, such as backup and data sharing between consumers.

How are usage fees calculated? Typically, based on the number of users, the time in use, per-execution, per-record-processed, network bandwidth consumed, and quantity/duration of data stored.

individually allocated to specific consumers, and paid for based on factors such as how long the units are retained, who has access to them, how they are used, etc. In the case of SaaS, what is being rented is access to an application [Sii01]. Typically, access to the application is over a network connecting the SaaS provider with the consumer. For public or outsourced SaaS, most application program logic is executed on the cloud provider's servers. The consumer's browser[11] provides: (1) the consumer interface that captures consumer keystrokes and other inputs, and produces output in the form of graphics/sound, and (2) the data export that outputs data to local storage devices such as USB devices or printers. To protect application data exchanged between the consumer's browser and the cloud provider over the network, cryptography is required. Typically, the consumer's browser and the cloud provider's server begin a session by first negotiating a shared key using one of several standard key exchange protocols (e.g., TLS[Die08] or SSL[Net96]). The consumer's browser and the cloud provider can then use the key to encrypt communications.[12] The consumer and provider can then exchange credentials to prove their

---

[11] The consumer may use a browser or other thin-client application to communicate with a SaaS cloud; in practice, browsers are often used as they require no additional installation. For simplicity, this document describes the consumer-side software simply as a "browser."

[12] This protection is not without risk however because past implementation errors or protocol flaws have enabled man-in-the-middle attacks that could allow an attacker to hijack a consumer's cloud resources [Mar09].

identities to one another. Generally, a consumer provides an account name and password or other authentication credential such as a time-based hardware token value.

The SaaS provider's main responsibility to the consumer is to ensure that the software that it supplies is solidly supported and tested. Another key requirement is that SaaS applications be scalable to increasingly larger consumer workloads. Maintaining an infrastructure to carry this out in a secure environment with specified uptime for the consumer is a critical aspect. Many consumers may have valuable organizational data stored in the cloud and some of this information may be proprietary and business-sensitive; therefore a secure environment is paramount.

The following six subsections describe several important characteristics of SaaS offerings: Abstract Interaction Dynamics; Software Stack and Provider/Consumer Scopes of Control; Benefits; Issues and Concerns; Candidate Application Classes; and Recommendations.

5.1   Abstract Interaction Dynamics

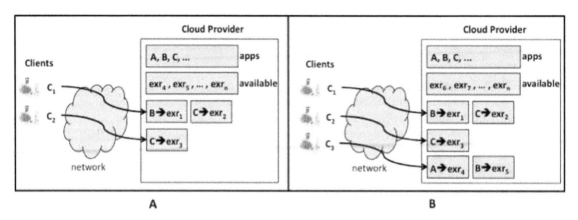

Figure 9: SaaS Consumer/Provider Interaction Dynamics

To provide an understanding of SaaS cloud offerings, this section abstractly describes the dynamics of an interaction between clients of a typical consumer and the SaaS cloud service through a simplified model. One such model is shown in Figure 9. Figure 9.A depicts a cloud providing services to two clients, C_1 and C_2. In a private cloud, the clients will belong to (or be associated with) a single consumer organization; in other deployment models, as covered in Section 4, the clients may represent different consumers. Abstractly, the cloud provider possesses an inventory of software applications ("apps" in the figure) that it is offering to clients for use over the network. In addition, the cloud provider possesses (or can rent) application execution resources (labeled "exr" in the figure). In Figure 9.A, client C_1 is currently using two applications, B and C. To execute the apps for client C_1, the cloud provider has allocated two execution resources, exr_1 and exr_2, with exr_1 supplying the processing power and other resources to run the B application (denoted by B→exr_1 in the figure), and exr_2 supplying the processing power and other resources to run the C application (denoted by C→exr_2 in the figure). An execution resource might be, e.g., a physical computer, a virtual machine (discussed in Section 7), or a running server program that can service client requests, start a virtual machine, or even rent computing cycles and storage from another organization. Similarly, client C_2, is using one application, C, which is supported by execution resource exr_3. Note that the same application (C in this case) can be rented out to multiple clients at the same time, as long as the cloud provider can marshal the execution resources to support the application. As shown in Figure 9.B, when an additional client requests applications from the cloud, the cloud provider allocates extra execution resources to support the requested applications.

5.2 Software Stack and Provider/Consumer Scope of Control

In SaaS, the cloud provider controls most of the software stack. Figure 10 illustrates how control and management responsibilities are shared. In the center, the figure depicts a traditional software stack comprising layers for the hardware, operating system, middleware, and application. The figure also depicts an assignment of responsibility either to the cloud provider, the cloud consumer, or both.

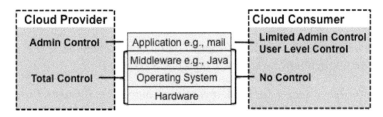

Figure 10: SaaS Provider/Consumer Scope of Control

In the SaaS service model, a consumer possesses control over the application-specific resources that a SaaS application makes available. For example, if a provider supplies an email application, the consumer will typically have the ability to create, send, and store email messages. Figure 10 depicts this as "user level" control. In some cases, a consumer also has limited administrative control of an application. For example, in the example of an email application, selected consumers may have the ability to create email accounts for other consumers, review the activities of other consumers, etc.

In contrast, a provider typically maintains significantly more administrative control at the application level. A provider is responsible for deploying, configuring, updating, and managing the operation of the application so that it provides expected service levels to consumers. A provider's responsibilities also extend to enforcing acceptable usage policies, billing, problem resolution, etc. To discharge these obligations a provider must exercise final authority over the application. Although a consumer may possess limited administrative control, the control possessed by the consumer exists only at the discretion of the provider.

The middleware layer depicted in Figure 10 provides software building blocks for the application. A middleware layer can take a number of forms, ranging from: (1) traditional software libraries, to (2) software interpreters (e.g., the Java Virtual Machine [Lind99] or the Python runtime environment [Pyt11] or implementations of the Common Language Infrastructure [ISO/IEC 23271:2006]), to (3) invocations of remote network services. Middleware components may provide database services, user authentication services, identity management, account management, etc. In general, a cloud consumer needs and possesses no direct access to this layer. Similarly, consumers require and generally possess no direct access to the operating system layer or the hardware layer. Optionally, a provider may employ a Virtual Machine Monitor (VMM) as part of the software stack. In this case (not shown in Figure 10), the VMM resides between the hardware and the operating-system layers. A VMM can be a useful tool to help a provider manage available hardware resources, however SaaS consumers do not require or generally possess direct access to it.

5.3 Benefits

Compared with traditional computing and software distribution solutions, SaaS clouds provide scalability and also shift significant burdens from consumers to providers, resulting in a number of opportunities for greater efficiency and, in some cases, performance. The following sections describe five key benefits of SaaS clouds.

5.3.1 Very Modest Software Tool Footprint

As browsers that are capable of efficiently displaying interactive content have become ubiquitous, SaaS application deployment has become increasingly convenient and efficient with little or no client-side software required. Several factors contribute to this value proposition:

- Unlike shrink-wrapped software applications, SaaS applications can be accessed without waiting for complex installation procedures.

- Because SaaS applications have very small footprints on client computers, risk of configuration interference between applications on client computers is reduced.

- Distribution costs for the software are fundamentally reduced. As discussed in [Cho06], lower distribution costs allow for economical development and deployment of software features even if they appeal to only a small portion of consumers.

5.3.2 Efficient Use of Software Licenses

License management overheads can be dramatically reduced using SaaS. As discussed in [Sii01], consumers can employ a single license on multiple computers at different times instead of purchasing extra licenses for separate computers that may not be used and thus over-provisioning the license. Additionally, traditional license management protocols and license servers are not needed to protect the intellectual property of application developers because the software runs in the provider's infrastructure and can be directly metered and billed.

5.3.3 Centralized Management and Data

For public and outsourced scenarios, the SaaS service model implies that the majority of the data managed by an application resides on the servers of the cloud provider. The provider may store this data in a decentralized manner for redundancy and reliability, but it is centralized from the point of view of consumers. This logical centralization of data has important implications for consumers. One implication is that, for public and outsourced scenarios, the SaaS provider can supply professional management of the data, including for example, compliance checking, security scanning, backup, and disaster recovery. When these services are provided away from the consumer's premises in public and outsourced scenarios, SaaS management of data gives consumers protection against the possibility of a single catastrophe destroying both the consumer's facility and data. This benefit, however, is contingent upon the SaaS provider protecting its facilities from catastrophic attack or other undesirable events. For on-site private and community SaaS clouds, the benefits of centralized management are similar however there is less resilience against catastrophic losses unless consumers explicitly plan for those contingencies. The "on demand" network access of SaaS applications also relieves consumers from the need to carry their data with them in some settings, thus potentially reducing risks from loss or theft. When supported by the application's logic, remote data management also facilitates sharing among other consumers.

5.3.4 Platform Responsibilities Managed by Providers

Generally, for outsourced or public SaaS clouds, consumers need not become involved with the management of a provider's infrastructure. For example, consumers need not be distracted by which operating system, hardware devices or configuration choices, or software library versions underlie a SaaS application. In particular, providers have responsibility for operational issues such as backups, system maintenance, security patches, power management, hardware refresh, physical plant security, etc. Providers also have an obligation to field services that guard against known exploits at the application level. Further, consumers are not required to maintain on premises IT support to perform these tasks, with an exception that on premises IT support is still necessary to connect consumer browsers securely to the network. Because SaaS providers implement new application features and provide the server side hardware that runs them, SaaS providers also have advantages in managing the introduction of new features while mitigating the need for consumers to upgrade their hardware systems to use the new features.

5.3.5 Savings in Up-front Costs

Outsourced and public SaaS clouds allow a consumer to begin using an application without the up-front costs of equipment acquisition, but potentially with a recurring usage fee. Additionally, cloud providers should be able to provision their hardware, power, and other computing resources at scale and more efficiently than individual consumers, which may reduce ongoing costs to consumers. This provides a basis for cost savings to consumers (assuming a competitive marketplace). As with any buy vs. rent decision, a careful analysis of all the cost considerations should be performed, including anticipated future prices, before committing to a single approach.

5.4 Issues and Concerns

Compared with traditional computing and software distribution solutions, outsourced and public SaaS clouds perform more application-level logic at provider facilities. For all scenarios, SaaS clouds place significant reliance on consumer browsers to be both reliable and secure. These constraints raise a number of issues and concerns, and affect the types of applications that are good fits for SaaS.

5.4.1 Browser-based Risks and Risk Remediation

Although browsers encrypt their communications with cloud providers, subtle disclosures of information are still possible. For example, the very presence or absence of message traffic, or the sizes of messages sent, or the originating locations may leak information that is indirect but still of importance to some consumers. Additionally, even strong cryptography can be weakened by implementation mistakes; a common mistake is to generate keys or passwords in a manner that reduces their strength, thus making the cryptography vulnerable to brute-force guessing attacks. Furthermore, man-in-the-middle attacks on the cryptographic protocols used by browsers [Mar09] can allow an attacker to hijack a consumer's cloud resources. These risks apply to non-cloud environments as well; however in cloud computing, the reliance upon safe, end-user, client applications and networking may be greater.

By relying on a consumer's browser for software application interfaces, the SaaS approach also raises a risk that, if a consumer visits a malicious Web site and the browser becomes contaminated, subsequent access to a SaaS application might compromise the consumer's data. Another risk is that data from different SaaS applications might be inadvertently mixed on consumer systems within consumer Web browsers. In Figure 9, for example, client C_1 is concurrently running applications B and C. Depending on the data processed by B and C, it may be important to keep them separated. Additionally, although Figure 9 depicts applications B and C as being served by the same provider, in other scenarios they may originate from different organizations and require careful separation. Prominent Web browsers provide features, such as sandboxes to separate Web pages (and the interactive code that they contain) from one another, but sandboxing relies on Web browsers' robust resistance to attack. Unfortunately, as is evidenced by numerous competitions [Por10, Mar09], Web browsers are often vulnerable to malicious Web sites. One work-around to this issue is for consumers to use multiple browsers and to dedicate specific browsers to important SaaS applications and not to perform general-purpose Web surfing that may expose them to attack. Another work-around is for consumers to use a virtual desktop when connecting to cloud-hosted applications, which provides a secure, fully functional work platform that is governed by strict policies for limiting what can or cannot be accessed elsewhere, while connected to a cloud.

5.4.2   Network Dependence

The availability of a SaaS application depends on a reliable and continuously available network. In the public SaaS cloud scenario, the network's reliability cannot be guaranteed either by the cloud consumer or by the cloud provider because the Internet is not under the control of either one. In outsourced private or community SaaS scenarios, network security and reliability can be achieved using dedicated, protected communications links, but at a cost. Although a SaaS application may include a "disconnected mode" for continued processing during network outages, the fundamental organization of SaaS, with application logic implemented on the cloud provider's servers, implies that the actual functionality of the application will be dependent on its ability to access a reliable network.

5.4.3   Lack of Portability between SaaS Clouds

Portability in SaaS is a concern for transitioning workloads from one SaaS cloud to another. Formats for exporting and importing data may not be fully compatible among SaaS clouds. Customized workflow and business rules, user interface and application settings, support scripts, data extensions, and add-ons developed over time can also be provider specific and not easily transferable.

5.4.4   Isolation vs. Efficiency (Security vs. Cost Tradeoffs)

The execution resources exr_1 ... exr_5 depicted in Figure 9 are abstract and raise questions of how SaaS application software is actually executed by a SaaS provider, and whether a SaaS provider has a fixed or variable ability to execute software for its consumers. Figure 11 provides a more concrete view of one way such execution can be accomplished (several options are discussed in [Cho08].

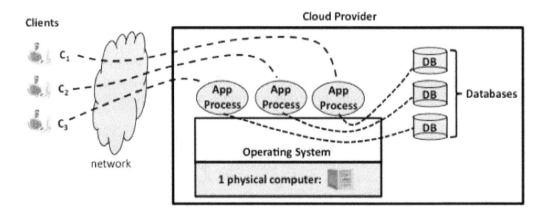

Figure 11: SaaS Isolation vs. Efficiency Favoring Isolation

In the scenario depicted in Figure 11, the cloud provider runs a separate instance (active copy) of the application for each client, and configures the application instances as necessary so that they can coexist on a single physical computer without interference. Since SaaS applications often store data on behalf of clients (or at least store configuration preferences), the figure also shows separate database systems connected to the separate application instances. Essentially, each client has a separate running copy of the application and a separate data store, and the separation between clients is provided by the operating system. Separation can be provided in numerous ways using the operating system, with various tradeoffs in the strength of the separation and the cost of implementing it. Higher confidence could be obtained by running applications in separate virtual machines or on separate physical computers, but those approaches are more expensive. Figure 11 allows a single physical machine to serve some number of clients simultaneously, but this approach is still expensive in that all the overhead costs of a separate copy of an application and a separate database must be incurred for each active client.

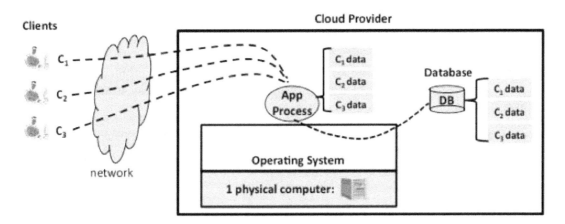

Figure 12: SaaS Isolation vs. Efficiency Favoring Efficiency

Figure 12 depicts a more efficient approach. In this approach, the provider reengineers the SaaS application to concurrently serve multiple clients and to save the data in a combined database. The separation between client processing and data in the approach shown in Figure 12 depends on careful engineering of the application since the application may be processing data belonging to multiple clients at a single time. Additionally, the application must manage scheduling issues to prevent the innocent or malevolent actions of one client from degrading the performance experienced by another. By sharing a single program and database in this manner, the approach of Figure 12 lowers costs for the provider (but at an increased security risk to consumers). It should be observed that there are a number of other potential engineering tradeoffs in how processing and data storage is implemented by a SaaS provider. For instance, many different SaaS applications could be concurrently implemented in a single unified application process and data storage system. Additionally, the actual computing resources (processes running on a physical computer) may be obtained in a variety of ways ranging from direct provision via the SaaS provider's data center to hardware rentals via an IaaS cloud provider. These different types of service configurations also affect the security of consumer workloads since they affect the mechanisms protecting consumer data and the locations where client programs and data reside. Additionally, portability of workloads requires a level of compatibility and interoperability between SaaS applications. A general discussion of engineering tradeoffs for a SaaS application is presented in [Cho08].

5.5 Candidate Application Classes

SaaS applications can work well when there is reliable, low-latency networking with adequate bandwidth to import and export expected quantities of consumer data (and assuming no malicious attacks, e.g., denial of service). The performance with respect to latency and data transfer speed varies depending on the type of application. For example, numerous SaaS service offerings exist in the following broad areas:

■ **Business logic.** Applications in this area connect businesses with their suppliers, employees, investors, and customers. Examples include invoicing, funds transfer, inventory management, and customer relationship management.

- **Collaboration.** Applications in this area help teams of people work together, either within or between organizations. Examples include calendar systems, email, screen sharing, collaborative document authoring, conference management, and online gaming.

- **Office productivity.** Applications in this area implement the applications that typify office environments such as word processors, spreadsheet programs, presentation programs, and database programs. In their SaaS incarnations, these applications often offer collaboration features missing from traditional office productivity applications.

- **Software tools.** Applications in this area solve security or compatibility problems and support new software development. Examples include format conversion tools, security scanning and analysis, compliance checking, and Web development.

It is important to emphasize that the SaaS deployment model is broadly applicable and spans more groupings of software than are enumerated above. As the ubiquity and performance of the Internet have increased, SaaS has become nearly universally applicable. There are, however, three classes of software that may not be good fits for public SaaS:

- **Real-time software.** Applications, such as flight control systems or factory robot control, that require precise timing of task completion, are unsuitable for SaaS because of the variable response times that SaaS systems may experience as well as the typically unavoidable round trip delays for messages to be exchanged between SaaS consumers and cloud providers.

- **Bulk-consumer-data.** For some applications, such as monitoring of medical devices or other physical phenomenon, data originates physically at the consumer and the volume of data can be extremely large. In such cases, it may not be feasible to transfer the data in real time over wide area networks to a SaaS provider.

- **Critical software.** Software is labeled critical if its failure can cause loss of life or loss of significant property. Critical software may fail either by doing the wrong thing or by doing the right thing too slowly (or too quickly). Achieving acceptable reliability for critical software is an area of ongoing research, but one of the key engineering approaches is to reduce the complexity of the critical software. By its nature, however, SaaS applications depend on the proper operation of a large and complex software stack that includes a network. In the case of a public SaaS, the network is not a controlled medium, and hence no guarantees can be given that the network will continue to provide acceptable levels of service.

It is possible that these issues can be ameliorated, however, with on-site SaaS, or with outsourced or community SaaS where explicit network provisioning has been performed to ensure network quality to the needed level of assurance.

Additionally, some applications require high refresh rates to the consumer's display. Although SaaS can support high refresh rates, the supportable refresh rate falls as the distance between the SaaS provider and the consumer increases. Historically, higher latencies experienced on long haul networks also imply that high refresh rates may not be achievable on a continuous basis.

5.6 Recommendations for Software as a Service

For Federal information systems and those operated on behalf of the US Government, the Federal Information Security Management Act of 2002 and the associated NIST standards and special publications (e.g. FIPS 199, FIPS 200, SP 800-53, etc.) do apply to SaaS systems. General recommendations for cloud computing services are given in section 9. See also Appendix A on the sharing of roles and responsibilities between customers and cloud providers. The following are additional recommendations for SaaS systems:

- **Data Protection.** Analyze the SaaS provider's data protection mechanisms, data location configuration and database organization/transaction processing technologies, and assess whether they will meet the confidentiality, compliance, integrity and availability needs of the organization that will be using the subscribed SaaS application.

- **Client Device/Application Protection.** Consistent with the FIPS 199 impact level of the data being processed, protect the cloud consumer's client device (e.g., a computer running a Web browser) so as to control the exposure to attacks.

- **Encryption.** Require that strong encryption using a robust algorithm with keys of required strength be used for Web sessions whenever the subscribed SaaS application requires the confidentiality of application interaction and data transfers. Also require that the same diligence be applied to stored data. Federal agencies must employ government-approved cryptographic algorithms for encryption and digital signature, and the implementations need to be FIPS 140-2 validated. Understand how cryptographic keys are managed and who has access to them. Ensure that cryptographic keys are adequately protected.

- **Secure Data Deletion.** Require that cloud providers offer a mechanism for reliably deleting data on a consumer's request.

6.   Platform-as-a-Service Cloud Environments

A Platform-as-a-Service (PaaS) cloud provides a toolkit for conveniently developing, deploying, and administering application software that is structured to support large numbers of consumers, process very large quantities of data, and potentially be accessed from any point in the Internet. PaaS clouds will typically provide a set of software building blocks and a set of development tools such as programming languages and supporting run-time environments that facilitate the construction of high-quality, scalable applications. Additionally, PaaS clouds will typically provide tools that assist with the deployment of new applications. In some cases, deploying a new software application in a PaaS cloud is not much more difficult than uploading a file to a Web server. PaaS clouds will also generally provide and maintain the computing resources (e.g., processing, storage, and networking) that consumer applications need to operate. In short, PaaS clouds are similar to any traditional computing system (i.e., platform) in that software applications can be developed for them and run on them.

PaaS

Who are the consumers?
1.   Application developers, who design and implement an application's software.
2.   Application testers, who run applications in various (possibly cloud-based) testing environments.
3.   Application deployers, who publish completed (or updated) applications into the cloud, and manage possible conflicts arising from multiple versions of an application.
4.   Application administrators, who configure, tune, and monitor application performance on a platform.
5.   Application end users, who subscribe to the applications deployed on a PaaS cloud: to end users, access to applications is the same as using a SaaS cloud.

What does the consumer get? The use of the PaaS cloud provider's tools and execution resources to develop, test, deploy and administer applications.

How are usage fees calculated? Typically, based on the number of consumers, the kind of consumers (e.g., developers vs. application end users), storage, processing, or network resources consumed by the platform, requests serviced, and the time the platform is in use.

Unlike the case of a traditional system, however, PaaS provides a basis for developers to create scalable applications. Applications for a public PaaS cloud can: (1) employ large quantities of computing resources as needed, (2) process large volumes of data as needed, (3) be deployed nearly instantly, (4) relieve consumers of numerous IT chores, and (5) be purchased incrementally, by paying ongoing usage fees instead of traditional up-front costs for equipment and IT staff training. Outsourced private or community PaaS clouds can provide similar abilities though the scale may be restricted depending on the outsourcing terms. For private or community non-outsourced PaaS clouds (see Sections 4.2 and 4.4), the scale is restricted by the data center resources.

The following six subsections describe several important characteristics of PaaS offerings: Abstract Interaction Dynamics; Software Stack and Provider/Consumer Scopes of Control; Benefits; Issues and Concerns; Candidate Application Classes; and Recommendations.

6.1   Abstract Interaction Dynamics

Figure 13 provides a simplified (four-step) view of the interaction dynamics of a PaaS cloud. Figure 13 A shows a PaaS cloud running two applications on behalf of a client, C_1. In Figure 13.A, the PaaS provider has a current inventory of three applications deployed ("apps"). The cloud provider also maintains a set of development tools ("dev tools" in the figure), and a set of execution environments ("exr" in the figure). As with the case of a SaaS provider as previously described in Section 5, an execution environment might be a physical computer, a virtual machine (discussed in Section 7), a running server program that can service client requests, the ability to start a virtual machine, or even the ability to rent computing cycles and storage from another organization. Figure 13.A also depicts two active applications, $B \rightarrow exr_1$ and $C \rightarrow exr_2$ indicating that applications B and C are using separate execution resources (just as they would in a SaaS environment).

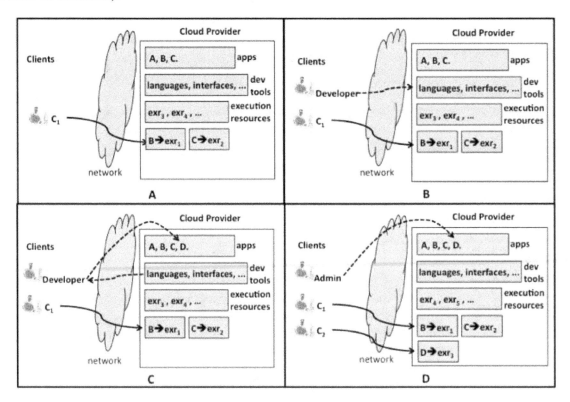

Figure 13: PaaS Consumer/Provider Interaction Dynamics

In Figure 13.B, a new developer client accesses the development tools of the provider. The development tools may include programming languages, compilers, interfaces, testing tools, and mechanisms to deploy an application once it's finished.

Figure 13.C illustrates the developer's use of tools. The developer may download tools and use them locally in the developer's infrastructure, or the developer may merely access tools in the provider's infrastructure. In either case, the output of the developer's actions is a new application, D, as shown in the figure, that is deployed into the provider's infrastructure.

In Figure 13.D, an administrator is shown configuring the new application that has been made available, and a new client, C_2, is shown using the new application.

Figure 13 provides a simplified view of how a PaaS cloud operates, however it illustrates key aspects of PaaS clouds: PaaS clouds are platforms for which software may be developed, onto which software may be deployed, and on which software may operate for its entire life cycle. There are many variations on this basic scenario. For instance, a developer may modify an existing application instead of creating a new application, and the normal phases of software development, including testing, version management, and decommissioning phases, are not shown.

6.2 Software Stack and Provider/Consumer Scope of Control

In PaaS, the cloud provider controls the more privileged, lower layers of the software stack. Figure 14 illustrates how control and management responsibilities are shared. In the center, the figure depicts a traditional software stack comprising layers for the hardware, operating system, middleware, and application. The figure also depicts an assignment of responsibility either to the cloud provider, the cloud consumer, or both.

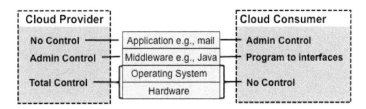

Figure 14: PaaS Component Stack and Scope of Control

The provider operates and controls the lowest layers, the operating system and hardware; implicit in this is control over networking infrastructure such as LANs and routers between data centers. At the middleware layer, the provider makes programming and utility interfaces available to the consumer; these interfaces provide the execution environment within which consumer applications run and provide access to needed resources such as CPU cycles, memory, persistent storage, data stores, data bases, network connections, etc. The provider determines the programming model, i.e., the circumstances under which consumer application code gets activated, and monitors the activities of consumer programs for billing and other management purposes. Once a consumer has used the facilities of the PaaS cloud to implement and deploy an application, the application essentially is a SaaS deployment as discussed in Section 5 and the consumer has administrative control over the application subject only to the provider supporting the consumer according to the terms of use, as discussed in Section 3.

6.3 Benefits

In the public and outsourced PaaS scenarios, a cloud provider is free to locate cloud infrastructure in low-cost areas, and consumers access cloud services over the open Internet. For all scenarios, by retaining control over the lower layers of the software stack as illustrated in Figure 14, PaaS providers are able to manage the lower layers and relieve PaaS consumers of the responsibility for selecting, installing, maintaining, or operating the platform components. Infrastructure charges are implicitly present in PaaS offerings because PaaS consumes infrastructure resources in some form, but the infrastructure charges are bundled in the rates charged for the PaaS execution environment resources (e.g., CPU, bandwidth, storage).

PasS shares many of the benefits of SaaS as discussed in Section 5.3:

■ Very Modest Software Tool Footprint (5.3.1),

■ Centralized Management and Data (5.3.3),

■ Platform Issues Managed by Providers (5.3.4), and

■ Savings in Up-front Costs (5.3.5).

6.3.1 Facilitated Scalable Application Development and Deployment

PaaS provides a low-cost way of developing and deploying applications. A variety of toolkits exist for developing PaaS applications and for supporting them both at the server side via data stores and server-side processing frameworks (e.g., [Msf11-2, Goo11, Sal11, Red10, Ama12]), and at the client side via thin clients and especially browser-based processing frameworks (e.g., [Gar05, Ado11, Goo11-2, Mic11, Dja11]). These techniques provide a way for organizations to develop and deploy enterprise applications and to maintain centralized control over their operation and the data that is processed with them. PaaS application development frameworks typically provide design patterns supporting a high level of scalability, thus enabling well-written PaaS applications to operate smoothly through large fluctuations in demand. In on-site scenarios, scalability will be limited to the resources provided by consumer data centers; however in outsourced scenarios more resources may be available at the providers' facilities and, particularly in the public scenario, well-written PaaS applications can be quickly deployed to large numbers of consumers and provide very large quantities of data and processing services.

6.4 Issues and Concerns

As with SaaS clouds discussed in Section 5, PaaS clouds, perform more application-level logic at provider facilities than do traditional computing solutions, and PaaS deployments also place significant burdens on consumer browsers (or thin clients) to maintain reliable and secure connections to provider systems and to maintain separation between different PaaS applications and accounts. PaaS clouds thus share SaaS issues and concerns as presented in Section 5.4):

- Browser-based Risks and Risk Remediation (5.4.1),

- Network Dependence (5.4.2), and

- Isolation vs. Efficiency (5.4.4).

In addition, several issues are specific to PaaS clouds.

6.4.1 Lack of Portability between PaaS Clouds

Portability in PaaS is a concern for new application development, particularly when platforms require proprietary languages and run-time environments. Even when standard languages are used, implementations of platform services may vary widely between providers – for example, one platform's file, queue, or hash-table interface may not be compatible with another's. Consumers creating new applications may mitigate portability risks by creating generalized interfaces to platform services instead of creating specialized implementations for specific platform providers. Such a strategy, however, incurs costs and also does not entirely mitigate the risks since a general interface that hides provider-specific variations will likely limit the use of provider-specific value added features, thus resulting in a "lowest common denominator" for application features.

6.4.2 Event-based Processor Scheduling

PaaS applications may be event driven with the events consisting of HTTP messages. This design is particularly cost effective in that, absent an outstanding request, few resources are consumed. However it poses resource constraints on applications, e.g., they must answer a request in a given time interval or they must continue a long-running request by queuing synthetic messages that then can be serviced. Also, tasks that execute quickly in a local application may not offer equivalent performance in a PaaS application.

6.4.3 Security Engineering of PaaS Applications

A PaaS application developer must manage a number of security exposures. Unlike the case of an application that can potentially run in an isolated environment using only local resources, PaaS applications access networks intrinsically. Additionally, PaaS applications must explicitly use cryptography, and must interact with the presentation features of common Web browsers that provide output to consumers. PaaS applications typically also require the use of multiple languages and formats, e.g., HTML, Java, JavaScript, XML, HTTP, .Net, and Web resource archive formats.

6.5 Candidate Application Classes

PaaS toolkits and services can be used to develop a wide variety of applications that can then be used as SaaS. The application classes that are good fits for PaaS are therefore essentially the same as those for SaaS, as presented in Section 5.5.

6.6 Recommendations for Platform as a Service

For Federal information systems and those operated on behalf of the US Government, the Federal Information Security Management Act (FISMA) of 2002 and the associated NIST standards and special publications (e.g. FIPS 199, FIPS 200, SP 800-53, etc.) do apply to PaaS systems. General recommendations for cloud computing services are given in section 9. See also Appendix A on the sharing of roles and responsibilities between customers and cloud providers. The following are additional recommendations for PaaS systems:

- **Generic Interfaces.** Before a decision is made to develop new applications on a public PaaS cloud platform, it is recommended to evaluate whether the application infrastructure interfaces (for file, queue, hash table, etc.) provided in that platform are or could be made generic enough to support portability and interoperability of the application. PaaS clouds that support generic interfaces are preferable.

- **Standard Languages and Tools.** Choose PaaS systems that work with standardized languages and tools unless the only practical options are PaaS systems that are restricted to proprietary languages and tools.

- **Data Access.** Choose PaaS systems that work with standard data access protocols (e.g., SQL) when practicable.

- **Data Protection.** Analyze the PaaS provider's data protection mechanisms, data location configuration and database organization/transaction processing technologies, and assess whether they will meet the confidentiality, compliance, integrity and availability needs of the organization that will be using the subscribed PaaS application.

- **Application Frameworks.** If available, choose PaaS systems that provide application development frameworks that include an architecture and tools for mitigating security vulnerabilities.

- **Component Testing.** Before a decision is made to deploy a new application on a public PaaS cloud platform (or in some cases composing an application from the building blocks provided by the PaaS cloud provider), ensure that software libraries included in the compilation phase or called during the execution phase behave as intended both in terms of functionality and performance.

- **Security.** Ensure that a PaaS application can be configured to run in a secure manner (e.g., a dedicated VLAN segment, using cryptography for client-server communications) and can be integrated with existing enterprise/agency security frameworks such as identification and authorization so that enterprise/agency security policies can be enforced.

■ **Secure Data Deletion.** Require that a cloud provider offer a mechanism for reliably deleting data on a consumer's request.

7.   Infrastructure-as-a-Service Cloud Environments

The purpose of this section is to describe the architecture and basic operation of Infrastructure as a Service (IaaS) clouds. This information is important for readers who need to evaluate whether IaaS clouds can satisfy particular reliability, compliance, and security requirements, as well as understand operational mechanisms. It is important to remember, however, that most public cloud implementations are proprietary, and thus their operational details are not publically available.

IaaS

Who are the consumers?

   System administrators.

What does a consumer get?

   Access to virtual computers, network-accessible storage, and network infrastructure components such as firewalls, and configuration services.

How are usage fees calculated?

   Typically, per cpu hour, data GB stored per hour, network bandwidth consumed, network infrastructure used (e.g., IP addresses) per hour, value-added services used (e.g., monitoring, automatic scaling).

The technical information contained in this section is a distillation of information from three sources: (1) openly published technical work on base technologies such as hardware virtualization [Pop74] that some cloud providers have publically acknowledged that they leverage, (2) inferences from openly published cloud system interfaces (e.g., [Ama10, Ama06]), and (3) insights from several Open Source cloud projects that have made design documentation and source code available (e.g., [Can11, Nas10, War09]). As such, this section describes how IaaS clouds operate in general and not specific terms. Note that this section refers to specific cloud computing projects by name, but these references do not constitute endorsements.

The following six subsections describe several important characteristics of IaaS offerings: Abstract Interaction Dynamics; Software Stack and Provider/Consumer Scopes of Control; an Operational View of an IaaS cloud; Benefits; Issues and Concerns; and Recommendations.

7.1   Abstract Interaction Dynamics

Figure 15 presents a simplified view of the interactions within an IaaS cloud. Figure 15.A depicts clients interacting with an IaaS cloud over a network. The provider has a number of available virtual machines (vm's) that it can allocate to clients. In the figure, client A has access to vm_1 and vm_2, and client B has access to vm_3. The provider retains vm_4 through vm_n, where it is presumed that n is larger than the number of vms any client is expected to request. Figure 15.B shows the situation just after a new client, C, has requested and received access to three more vms. At this point, client C has access to vm_4, vm_5 and vm_6, and the provider now retains only vm_7 through vm_N. Figure 15 is admittedly an extreme simplification of how an IaaS cloud really works, but it is still sufficient to illustrate a number of technical issues that must be addressed for an IaaS cloud to function. Further, Figure 15 only illustrates virtual machine allocation (by a provider) and interaction (by a consumer). Although it would be possible to build an IaaS cloud that provides only simple virtual machines that reset to default values when released, such a cloud would have limited functionality. Practical IaaS cloud systems also provide persistent data storage and stable network connectivity. They must also track resources that have economic cost, and bill those costs to consumers.

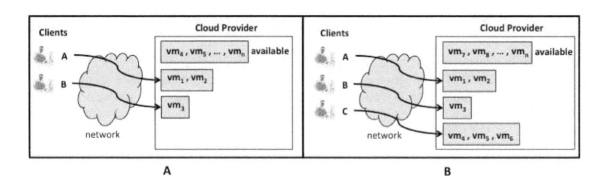

Figure 15: IaaS Provider/Consumer Interaction Dynamics

7.2   Software Stack and Provider/Consumer Scope of Control

In IaaS, the cloud provider controls the most privileged, lower layers of the software stack. Figure 16 illustrates how control and management responsibilities are shared. In the center, the figure depicts a traditional software stack comprising layers for the hardware, operating system, middleware, and applications. In the case of IaaS, the layer usually occupied by the operating system is split into two layers. The lower (and more privileged) layer is occupied by the Virtual Machine Monitor (VMM), which is also called the hypervisor. A hypervisor uses the hardware to synthesize one or more Virtual Machines (VMs); each VM is "an efficient, isolated duplicate of a real machine" [Pop73]. In essence, when a consumer rents access to a VM, the VM appears to the consumer as actual computer hardware that can be administered (e.g., powered on/off, peripherals configured) via commands sent over a network to the provider. An operating system running within a VM is called a guest operating system; when full virtualization techniques (see NIST SP 800-125) are used by the provider, the consumer is free (using the provider's utilities) to load any supported operating system software desired into the VM.

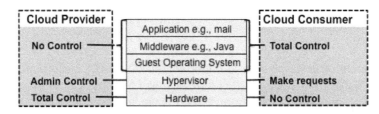

Figure 16: IaaS Component Stack and Scope of Control

As shown in Figure 16, the provider maintains total control over the physical hardware and administrative control over the hypervisor layer. The consumer may make requests to the cloud (including the hypervisor layer) to create and manage new VMs but these requests are honored only if they conform to the provider's policies over resource assignment. Through the hypervisor, the provider will typically provide interfaces to networking features (such as virtual network switches) that consumers may use to configure custom virtual networks within the provider's infrastructure. The consumer will typically maintain complete control over the operation of the guest operating system in each VM, and all software layers above it. While this structure grants very significant control over the software stack to consumers, consumers consequently must take on the responsibility to operate, update, and configure these traditional computing resources for security and reliability. This structure contrasts significantly with SaaS and PaaS clouds where many of these issues are handled transparently for consumers.

7.3 Operational View

Proprietary cloud providers do not release detailed technical information about their system architectures or algorithms; however, three Open Source systems (Ubuntu Enterprise Cloud [War09], NASA Nebula [Nas10], Eucalyptus [Nur08, Nur08-2], all based on the Eucalyptus source code provide detailed technical information about specific system architectures.[13] This section presents a logical view of IaaS cloud structure and operation. This logical view has been substantially informed by documentation from the Eucalyptus and Ubuntu Enterprise Cloud projects;[14] however, the informal model presented here is more abstract and general. This model is based on intuitive constraints of the provisioning of IaaS cloud services: IaaS clouds must provide the resources described above with both performance and cost efficiency while maintaining centralized control and the capability to scale up without disrupting service. These constraints imply a natural three-level hierarchy in IaaS cloud systems, with the top level responsible for central control, the middle level responsible for management of possibly large computer clusters that may be geographically distant from one another, and the bottom level responsible for running the host computer systems on which virtual machines are created.

Figure 17 illustrates this layered and abstract model. At the top layer is the Cloud Manager with responsibility for user accounts and high-level allocation of resources within the overall cloud. At the mid-layer are Cluster Managers with responsibility over large numbers of computers and their interconnection, as well as local storage. At the bottom layer are the Computer Managers with responsibility over VMs running on individual computers. A specific implementation may split up and parallelize some components for performance reasons, may introduce more intermediary layers for additional coordination, or may locate storage on networks different from the ones indicated in the model.

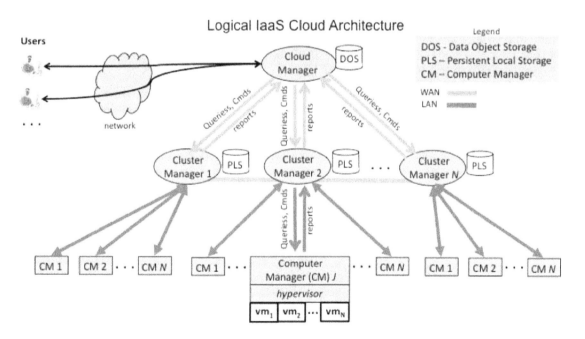

Figure 17: Local IaaS Cloud Architecture

IaaS clouds are computing systems for dynamic resource renting; consumer queries and commands generally flow into the system at the top and are forwarded down through the layers that either answer the queries or execute the commands. Status reports flow in the reverse direction back to the consumer.

---

[13] Other open source projects, some not based on Eucalyptus, are in progress as well.
[14] Note: this is not an endorsement of these projects.

Generally, the Cloud Manager and the Cluster Managers shown in Figure 17 will be connected by fast networks of IP routers: this reflects the need to add capacity in the form of new data centers as a cloud expands. Communications between Computer Managers, in contrast, tend to be local and very fast (e.g., 10GB Ethernet). While there is nothing to prevent all of the links in a cloud from being implemented in fast local networks, that approach is not scalable and makes a cloud vulnerable to local events that can disrupt service, e.g., natural disasters. Similarly, there is nothing to prevent a cloud from being completely dispersed over wide area links, but such a cloud could suffer a performance disadvantage.

The following subsections summarize the operation of the three main layers: the cloud manager, the cluster manager, and the computer manager.

7.3.1 Operation of the Cloud Manager

The Cloud Manager is the public access point to the cloud where consumers sign up for accounts, manage the resources they rent from the cloud, and access data stored in the cloud. The Cloud Manager includes mechanisms for authenticating consumers, and for generating or validating access credentials (e.g., cryptographic keys) that consumers then employ when communicating with their virtual machines. The Cloud Manager also performs top-level resource allocation; when a consumer issues a command to rent a number of resources, the Cloud Manager must determine if the cloud has enough free resources to satisfy the request, and if so, which Cluster Manager (or Managers) have some or all the resources. If the request can be satisfied, the Cloud Manager must commit to the allocation of the resources at the participating Cluster Managers, and must coordinate the setup of virtual networking so that the consumer can uniformly access all resources. The Cloud Manager will also enforce any cloud-global policies governing resource requests.

In addition to coordination with Cluster Managers, Figure 17 shows the Cloud Manager connected to the cloud's Data Object Storage (DOS) repository. In actual implementations, the DOS could be distributed or put on different networks; however, the DOS services need to be available both to running virtual machines in the cloud and to systems from outside the cloud, and must be coordinated sufficiently with the Cloud Manager to keep track of valid consumer identities both to allow their administrative actions in the DOS and for billing. These constraints imply a structure with close ties between the DOS and the Cloud Manager, and with wide-area network access from the DOS to both running virtual machines and external systems.

7.3.2 Operation of the Cluster Managers

Each Cluster Manager is responsible for the operation of a collection of computers that are connected via high speed local area networks. A computer cluster may contain hundreds or thousands of computers. A Cluster Manager receives resource allocation commands and queries from the Cloud Manager, and calculates whether part or all of a command can be satisfied using the resources of the computers in the cluster. A Cluster Manager queries the Computer Managers for the computers in the cluster to determine resource availability, and returns messages to the Cloud Manager on whether part, or all, of a request can be satisfied in a cluster. If subsequently directed by the Cloud Manager, a Cluster Manager then instructs the Computer Managers to perform resource allocation, and reconfigures the virtual network infrastructure to give the consumer uniform access.

In addition to being connected to individual computers via LAN links, Figure 17 shows each Cluster Manager also connected to Persistent Local Storage (PLS). As discussed above, virtual machines need persistent disk-like storage to preserve their work while virtual machines are de-allocated and later reallocated. The most natural location for this storage is where very high speed connections to virtual machines are available, but where the storage is not permanently bound to any specific computer system.

7.3.3 Operation of the Computer Managers

At the lowest layer in the hierarchy, a Computer Manager cooperates with the hypervisor that runs on each computer system in a cluster. In response to queries from its Cluster Manger, a Computer Manager returns status information including how many virtual machines are running and how many can still be started. In response to commands issued from its Cluster Manager, a Computer Manager uses the command interface of its hypervisor to start, stop, suspend, and reconfigure virtual machines, and to set the local virtual network configuration. With some hypervisor technologies, network packets exchanged between different virtual machines running on the same hypervisor can be implemented using very high performance in-memory messages, thus boosting performance. The Computer Manager is responsible for configuring such optimizations. As noted above, virtual machines running on behalf of different consumers must appear to be isolated from one another; the Computer Manager on each computer system is responsible for using the facilities of its hypervisor to generate this useful illusion to the greatest extent possible.

As illustrated in Figure 17, the operation of an IaaS cloud is a cyclical process of consumer requests flowing in and down through the hierarchy, and responses flowing back up to consumers. In addition to virtual machine operations, consumers may directly access data storage servers in the cloud. Even though the aggregate consumer demand peaks and troughs should be more gradual than individual consumer demand peaks and troughs, the cloud will sometimes be underutilized and migration of consumer workloads from computer system to computer system, or even from cluster to cluster, is a strategy that can concentrate consumer workloads on a set of highly utilized machines and allow others to be turned off to save some of the costs of their operation or to allow maintenance activities to be performed. Although Figure 17 shows a static structure of computer systems and networks, in reality physical hardware wears out or fails, and the cloud's structure and algorithms must allow for its replacement without wide-scale service interruptions. Note that the underlying mobility of virtual machines is an important tool for accommodating the inevitable need for hardware replacement. In addition, providers can use virtualization to transparently add new capacity in the form of additional computers within clusters or additional clusters to accommodate growth in demand for cloud services.

7.4 Benefits

As with SaaS and PaaS clouds, in the public and outsourced IaaS scenarios, a cloud provider is free to locate cloud infrastructure in low-cost areas and have consumers access cloud services over the open Internet; cost savings from lower cost infrastructure may be shared with consumers in the form of lower service charges. Furthermore, public and outsourced IaaS clouds allow for savings in up-front costs as do public or outsourced PaaS and SaaS clouds:

■ Savings in Up-front Costs (5.3.5).

In general, IaaS places more system management responsibility on consumers than either SaaS or PaaS; consumers need to manage the VMs and virtualized infrastructure and need to perform system administrator work. Although the provider may offer carefully constructed operating system images and services, replicated storage, cryptography, firewalls, monitoring, demand-based automated VM startup/shutdown, etc., responsibility for the operation of all software layers above the hypervisor rests primarily with the consumer. This can be considered as either a benefit or a concern, depending on the consumer's skill set and special needs.

The following sections discuss key benefits.

7.4.1 Full Control of the Computing Resource Through Administrative Access to VMs

Consumer access to IaaS cloud resources is typically performed through standard network protocols that use cryptography to prevent eavesdropping or tampering by third parties. Access to cloud resources over the network takes essentially three distinct forms: (1) a consumer issues administrative commands to the cloud provider, such as requests to run virtual machines or to save data on the cloud's servers, (2) a consumer with administrative access to specific running virtual machines (i.e., the consumer who is currently renting them) issues administrative commands to the virtual machines, such as starting a Web server on a virtual machine or installing a new application, and (3) any user, and possibly an anonymous user, with access to the public network interacts with the virtual machines using the network services running on the virtual machines that a consumer has previously enabled. As an example, for a UNIX-like virtual machine, the consumer with administrative access typically has an administratively privileged account that is accessed via a network protocol such as Secure Shell [Ylo06].

7.4.2 Flexible, Efficient Renting of Computing Hardware

Fundamentally, cloud computing provides rental of computing resources. These resources, which are typically accessed by consumers over a network, must be measurable in units that can be individually allocated to specific consumers, and paid for based on the length of time a consumer retains a resource. In the case of an IaaS cloud, the primary units of allocation are (administrative access to) VMs, network bandwidth, storage, and IP addresses. Additional resources include monitoring services, firewalls, synchronization mechanisms such as queues, databases, etc. A powerful aspect of having administrative access to a VM is that a consumer can run almost any software the consumer desires, including a custom operating system.

In addition to providing the functionality of raw hardware access, public and outsourced IaaS clouds provide the ability to quickly rent and then release large numbers of VMs or other cloud resources. This gives a consumer the ability to quickly set up large networks of VMs running consumer-selected software to solve large problems without incurring the expense of purchasing and maintaining the necessary hardware.

7.4.3 Portability, Interoperability with Legacy Applications

Because IaaS clouds allow consumers to install and run operating systems of their choosing, a high level of compatibility can be maintained between legacy applications and workloads in an IaaS cloud. For example, nearly any conventional network application (e.g., Web server, email server, database) that a consumer normally runs on consumer-owned server hardware can be run from VMs in an IaaS cloud. Furthermore, many user-facing applications can also be run in an IaaS cloud by virtual desktop technology. While many applications can readily be ported to VMs, however, not all applications can be. For example, applications that require specialized hardware support are not ideal candidates for porting.

7.5 Issues and Concerns

As with PaaS and SaaS clouds discussed in Section 5, IaaS clouds depend on a secure and reliable network, and also often depend on a secure and reliable browser for account administration.

▪ Network Dependence (5.4.2), and

▪ Browser-based Risks and Risk Remediation (5.4.1).

In addition, several issues are specific to IaaS clouds.

7.5.1 Compatibility with Legacy Security Vulnerabilities

By allowing consumers to run legacy software systems in the providers' infrastructures, IaaS clouds expose consumers to all of the security vulnerabilities of those legacy software systems.

7.5.2 Virtual Machine Sprawl

IaaS systems allow consumers to create and potentially retain many VMs in various states, e.g., running, suspended, and off. An inactive VM can easily become out of date with respect to important security updates; if an out-of-date VM is activated, such a VM may become compromised. Although, in principle, a provider could update inactive VMs on behalf of consumers, the mechanics of such updating are complex, and the maintenance of security updates typically is a consumer responsibility.

7.5.3 Verifying Authenticity of an IaaS Cloud Provider Web Site

Although the features outlined in Section 7.2 enable establishment of a secure session with IaaS cloud provider resources, the onus for verifying the identity of the provider's Web site still rests with the consumer through some means, e.g., checking with a third party credential service. The consumer's browser will typically use public key cryptography [Mar08, Die08] to establish a private link to the cloud provider, but it is a consumer's responsibility to check the identity of the cloud Web site to ensure that the private link is not with an imposter.

7.5.4 Robustness of VM-level Isolation

As Figure 15 illustrates, virtual machines are allocated for different consumers from a common pool. Consumers must be protected from potential eavesdropping or tampering on the part of other, possibly malicious, consumers. That is, consumers must be isolated from one another except to the extent that they choose to interact. An IaaS cloud typically uses a hypervisor (which is a software layer), in combination with hardware support for virtualization (e.g., AMD-V and Intel VT-x), to split each physical computer into multiple virtual machines. Isolation of the virtual machines depends on the correct implementation and configuration of the hypervisor. Hardware virtualization [Per08] provided by hypervisors has become a widely used technique for providing isolated, or sandboxed, computing environments, but the strength of the isolation in the presence of sophisticated attackers is an open research question.

7.5.5 Features for Dynamic Network Configuration for Providing Isolation

It is not evident from Figure 15, but the network infrastructure (e.g., routers, cables, network bandwidth, etc.) that supports each running VM is also allocated from a common pool of networking resources. When a VM is allocated by a cloud for a consumer, a network path through the cloud provider's infrastructure must be configured to allow that VM to communicate with the originating consumer and possibly also with arbitrary external entities on the Internet. To prevent undesirable interactions between consumers, the cloud network must prevent a consumer from observing any packets sent in the cloud by other consumers, and must also reserve sufficient bandwidth to ensure that each consumer has the expected level of service. VMs typically are dynamically allocated in only a few minutes, and the corresponding network configuration must be performed just as quickly. A number of techniques, such as Virtual Local Area Networks (VLANs) and overlay networks, provide a logical view of a network's topology that can be quickly reconfigured. Careful configuration of these features (and perhaps support in hypervisors as well) is required to prevent interference between networks belonging to different consumers.

7.5.6   Data Erase Practices

Virtual machines access disk resources maintained by the provider. When a consumer releases such a resource, the provider must ensure that the next consumer to rent the resource does not observe data residue from previous tenants. Strong data erase policies (e.g., multiple overwriting of disk blocks) are time consuming and may not be compatible with high performance when tenants are changing. Data replication and backup practices also complicate data erase practices.

7.6   Recommendations for Infrastructure as a Service

For Federal information systems and those operated on behalf of the US Government, the Federal Information Security Management Act (FISMA) of 2002 and the associated NIST standards and special publications (e.g. FIPS 199, FIPS 200, SP 800-53, etc.) do apply to IaaS systems. General recommendations for cloud computing services are given in section 9. See also Appendix A on the sharing of roles and responsibilities between customers and cloud providers. The following are additional recommendations for IaaS systems:

■ **Multi-tenancy.** When an IaaS cloud provider provides computing resources in the form of Virtual Machines (VMs), ensure that the provider has mechanisms in place to protect VMs from attacks (a) from other VMs on the same physical host (b) from the physical host as well as (c) from network originated attacks. Typical attack detection and prevention mechanisms include Virtual Firewalls, Virtual IDS/IPS, and Virtual Private Networks.

■ **Data Protection.** Analyze the IaaS provider's data protection mechanisms, data location configuration and processing technologies, and assess whether they will meet the confidentiality, compliance, integrity and availability needs of the organization that will be using the provider's infrastructure.

■ **Secure Data Deletion.** Require that a cloud provider offer a mechanism for reliably deleting data on a consumer's request.

■ **Administrative Access.** When renting computing resources from an IaaS cloud provider in the form of virtual machines or physical servers, ensure that a limited set of trained/trusted users (from the consumer organization) alone are provided administrative access to those resources.

■ **VM Migration.** Formulate a strategy for future migration of Virtual Machines and their associated storage among alternate cloud providers (e.g., the OVF standard could be a partial basis for such a strategy).

■ **Virtualization Best Practices.** Follow best practices for the administration of conventional systems and networks, and for use of virtualization (i.e., NIST Guide to Security for Full Virtualization Technologies SP 800-125).

8. Open Issues

Cloud computing is not a solution for all consumers of IT services, nor is it appropriate for all applications. As an emerging technology, cloud computing contains a number of issues, not all of which are unique to cloud, that are concerns for all IT hosted services. The purpose of this section is make the reader aware of how cloud computing relates to open issues in both locally-managed and outsourced IT computing services.

Some of these issues are traditional distributed computing topics that have remained open for decades but have now become more relevant because of the emergence of cloud computing. Other issues appear to be unique to cloud computing.

Complex computing systems are prone to failure and security compromise. Moreover, software that must accommodate complex requirements such as concurrency, dynamic configuration, and large scale computations, may exhibit higher defect densities than typical commercial grade software. With this in mind, it is important to understand that cloud systems, like all complex computing systems, will contain flaws, experience failures, and experience security compromises. This does not disqualify cloud systems from performing important work, but it does mean that techniques for detecting failures, understanding their consequences, isolating their effects, and remediating them, are central to the wide-scale adoption of clouds.

Cloud computing has potential to foster more efficient markets through swift leasing of computing resources. In some scenarios, cloud computing offers consumers the ability to forgo capital expenses (e.g., building internal computing centers) in exchange for variable service fees. Thus clouds offer consumers potential decreases in IT cash outflow. From a provider's perspective, cloud computing allows capital expenses to be leveraged into positive revenue streams after initial investments are made. These are familiar economic concepts that become mixed with the complexities of network and system configurations as well as the normal risks from exposing data and software assets to any external party.

The technical means of providing the quality of service promised by clouds are usually not disclosed to the consumer, thus raising questions about how consumers can verify that the promised quality of service has been provided. Additionally, efficient markets rely on consumers' ability to practically compare service offerings. This is difficult since service agreements do not all adhere to standard metrics, terminology, and vocabularies.

In summary, cloud computing raises a variety of issues that are grouped below into five areas in the remainder of this section: Computing Performance (Section 8.1), Cloud Reliability (Section 8.2), Economic Goals (Section 8.3), Compliance (Section 8.4), and Information Security (Section 8.5).

8.1 Computing Performance

Different types of applications require differing levels of system performance. For example, email is generally tolerant of short service interruptions, but industrial automation and real-time processing generally require both high performance and a high degree of predictability. Cloud computing incurs several performance issues that are not necessarily dissimilar from performance issues of other forms of distributed computing, but that are worth noting here.

8.1.1 Latency

Latency is the time delay that a system experiences when processing a request. Latency experienced by cloud consumers typically includes at least one Internet round-trip time, i.e., the time it takes for a request message to travel to a provider plus the time it takes for the response message to be received by a consumer. Generally, Internet round-trip times are not a single expected number but instead a range, with a significant amount of variability caused by congestion, configuration error, or failures. These factors are often not under the control of a provider or consumer. However, wide area network optimization technologies and web application acceleration services exist that may be employed to mitigate unacceptable performance. The suitability of an application for such an environment requires a careful analysis of the application's criticality, its built-in tolerance for variations in network service response times, and possible remediation(s) that can be applied after the fact. Note that this last statement is not unique to clouds.

8.1.2 Off-line Data Synchronization

Access to documents stored in clouds is problematic when consumers do not have network connectivity. The ability to synchronize documents and process data, while the consumer is offline and with documents stored in a cloud, is desirable, especially for SaaS clouds. Accomplishing such synchronization may require version control, group collaboration, and other synchronization capabilities within a cloud.

8.1.3 Scalable Programming

Programming "in the large" using toolkits such as MapReduce [Dea04], BigTable [Cha06], or even scalable queue services requires a new examination of application development practices. The ability to dynamically request additional computing capacity brings well-researched computing models such as grid computing and parallel processing out of scientific research labs and into more general computing usage. Cloud users can leverage data- and task-parallelism to take advantage of additional computing capacity, as well as to better scale computationally intensive tasks. Applications will likely, however, need to be reengineered to realize the full benefits of the new computing capacity that is now available on demand.

8.1.4 Data Storage Management

When data storage is considered in the context of clouds, consumers require the ability to: (1) provision additional storage capacity on demand, (2) know and restrict the physical location of the stored data, (3) verify how data was erased, (4) have access to a documented process for securely disposing of data storage hardware, and (5) administer access control over data. These are all challenges when data is hosted by an external party.

8.2 Cloud Reliability

Reliability refers to the probability that a system will offer failure-free service for a specified period of time within the bounds of a specified environment. For the cloud, reliability is broadly a function of the reliability of four individual components: (1) the hardware and software facilities offered by providers, (2) the provider's personnel, (3) connectivity to the subscribed services, and (4) the consumer's personnel.

Note that measuring the reliability of a specific cloud by the provider or consumer will be difficult for two main reasons. Firstly, a cloud may be a composition of various components, each inheriting a particular degree of reliability when it was measured as a standalone entity. When these components are combined, the resulting reliability is difficult to predict and may wind up being too course-grained. Secondly, reliability measurement is a function of an environment, and it may not be possible to fully understand the entire environment in which a cloud operates. As stated, the traditional definition of reliability is based on a context (environment) and a specified period of time for expected failure-free operation. For clouds, and most systems of significant scale, each component has a specific reliability given a specific context, and therefore understanding the union of the contexts is complex and possibly intractable.

8.2.1 Network Dependence

Cloud computing, as well as most enterprise applications, depends on network connectivity. For most clouds, the Internet must be continuously available for a consumer to access services. If a consumer is hosting a public network service using a provider, this dependence is similar to normal hosting in that supporting public network services are often accessed over the Internet. In the case of consumer-facing applications (e.g., webmail) entrusted to a cloud, this dependence is a risk whenever applications need continuous service. In numerous instances, consumer-facing applications either cannot access a cloud because of coverage limitations (e.g., subways, airplanes, remote locations) or are vulnerable to network disruption.

Network dependence implies that every application is a network application which suggests that the application is relatively complex: i.e., the risk of errors or security vulnerabilities will be higher than for non-networked, standalone applications. For example, cloud applications should typically cryptographically sign requests to providers and cryptographically protect consumer data in transit. In addition to normal outages or no-coverage zones, this dependence makes the application's normal operation sensitive to: (1) the health of the Internet's routing and naming infrastructure, (2) contention for local networking resources, and (3) force majeure events.

There have been several well-publicized regional Internet outages that have been the result of denial of service attacks, viruses infiltrating web servers, worms taking down DNS servers, failures in undersea cables, and fiber optic cables being damaged during earthquakes and subsequent mudslides. Although these outages are relatively infrequent, they can have an impact on network connectivity for hours. Contingency planning for these rare but often serious outages should be addressed as part of any organization's tactical IT plans. Most substantial applications are using the Internet today regardless of whether cloud computing is employed; therefore the reader should not assume that by avoiding a cloud a user automatically avoids risks associated with Internet outages.

8.2.2 Cloud Provider Outages

In spite of clauses in service agreements implying high availability and minimal downtimes for consumers, service or utility outages are inevitable due to man-made causes (e.g., malicious attacks or inadvertent administrator errors) or natural causes (e.g., floods, tornados, etc.).

Issues to be considered by consumers with regard to outages should be based on frequency of outages and expected recovery times. The two main considerations are:

■ What is the frequency and duration of outages that the consumer can tolerate without adversely impacting their business processes?

■ What are the resiliency alternatives a consumer has for contingency situations involving a prolonged outage?

8.2.3 Safety-Critical Processing

Safety-critical systems, both hardware and software, are a class of systems that are usually regulated by government authorities. Examples are systems that control avionics, nuclear materials, and medical devices. Such systems typically incur risks for a potential of loss of life or loss of property.

Such systems inherit "pedigree" as a byproduct of the regulations under which they are controlled, developed, and tested. Because of the current lack of ability to assess "pedigree" of one of these systems within a cloud (due to many distinct subcomponents that comprise or support the cloud), employing cloud technologies as the host for this class of applications is not recommended. However this does not suggest that for the development of safety-critical systems, cloud technologies should not be considered in supporting roles (e.g., employing a cloud to run a simulation of a safety-critical system under development).

More information on high-impact systems can be found in NIST FIPS 199.

8.3 Economic Goals

In public and outsourced scenarios, cloud computing offers an opportunity for consumers to use computing resources with small or modest up-front costs; furthermore, cloud computing promotes business agility by reducing the costs of pilot efforts, and may reduce costs to consumers through economies of scale. Although the benefits can be substantial, a number of economic risks must be considered as well.

8.3.1 Risk of Business Continuity

With on premises systems, consumers can continue to use products, even when the vendors have suspended support or have gone out of business. However for public or outsourced cloud computing, consumers depend on near real-time provisioning of services by providers. Since business shutdown is normal in any marketplace, this dependence is a risk to consumers with time-critical computing needs. Various approaches may be used to mitigate this risk, e.g., by employing redundant clouds, by monitoring the business health of providers, or by employing hybrid clouds.

8.3.2 Service Agreement Evaluation

As presented in Section 3, service agreements may define terms such as availability and security in specific and limited ways. Additionally, service agreements often place differing responsibilities on consumers to track changes in service agreements and to determine when to reevaluate service agreements.

Consumers need practical techniques to evaluate and compare service agreements. Currently, service agreements are human-generated and human-consumed. The commonality observed in current service agreement offerings, however, suggests that a basis exists for partial standardization of service agreement terminology. An open issue is how to design a service agreement template that would practically embody common service agreement terms. The specification of such templates could allow service agreements to be partially evaluated mechanically, thus reducing costs to consumers and increasing understanding into actual cloud service offerings.

Expressing service agreements in a machine-readable format using common ontologies might be a productive step in supporting automated evaluation of terms and conditions. A template defining common elements could support a query interface allowing potential consumers to quickly check and compare important components before investing the effort of manual evaluation of detailed terms and conditions. This then would support a more efficient cloud marketplace. The template could include standardized performance metrics that would allow consumers to compare service offerings in an objective manner.

8.3.3 Portability of Workloads

An initial barrier to cloud adoption is the need to move local workloads into a provider's infrastructure. For a consumer, this decision is less risky if a provider offers a practical method to move workloads (e.g., data workload or a fully encapsulated compute/storage/network workload) back to a consumer's premises on demand. Another issue is that a consumer should be able to move a workload from one provider to another on demand. These two needs would support a competitive cloud marketplace.

Portability relies on standardized interfaces and data formats. Cloud computing relies on both consensus and de facto standards such as TCP/IP, XML, WSDL, IA-64, x509, PEM, DNS, SSL/TLS, SOAP, REST, etc. Cloud service offerings that rent traditional computing resources (such as virtual machines or disk storage, i.e., IaaS) are closely related to existing standards, and hence some usage scenarios illustrating portability can be expressed using existing standards terminology.

Achieving portability is (and will remain) a challenge, because IaaS systems expose low-level details such as device interfaces, and any mismatch between such interfaces is an obstacle. In contrast, cloud service offerings that rent synthetic entities, such as access to a middleware stack (PaaS) or rights to use a given application (SaaS), are less well described by current standards, and hence even common terminology is lacking for describing how such entities might be transferred from one provider to another. While some low level details such as device interfaces are hidden by providers and thus helpful for mobility, the resource definitions are frequently vendor-specific.

8.3.4 Interoperability between Cloud Providers

For operations such as transferring a virtual machine image and data between providers, standardized formats for the data being transferred, billing, and identity management are needed. Some standards, such the Open Virtualization Format [DMT09] and the Cloud Data Management Interface [SNI10], have already been developed, but further development and experience is needed to reduce the costs of interoperation among providers. As a security example, a provider must be able to offer proper credentials to another provider before a transfer of consumer assets can be accomplished after a consumer requests the transfer. Further, once legitimacy is determined, the formats for the transferred objects must be compatible.

8.3.5 Disaster Recovery

Disaster recovery involves both physical and electronic mishaps with consumer assets. For natural disasters, replication of data at geographically distributed sites is advisable. For other physical disasters such as hardware theft, law enforcement involvement may offer the only remedy. For electronic mishaps, fault tolerance approaches such as redundancy, replication, and diversity are all applicable, depending on what type of electronic mishap is being protected against. Disaster recovery plans are applicable to all hosted IT services and should be documented and quickly executable. All of these traditional issues are complicated as consumers may not know where their workloads are hosted.

8.4 Compliance

When data or processing is moved to a cloud, the consumer retains the ultimate responsibility for compliance but the provider (having direct access to the data) may be in the best position to enforce compliance rules. A number of issues complicate compliance and should be addressed contractually. NIST and other US government agencies are evolving paths to help consumers with compliance issues, e.g., FEDRAMP [Fed10]. Also, see Section 3 and Appendix A.

8.4.1 Lack of Visibility

Consumers may lack visibility into how clouds operate. If so, they will likely be unable to tell if their services are being undertaken and delivered in a secure manner. Different models of cloud service delivery add or remove different levels of control from the consumer and provide different degrees of visibility. However, the option for a consumer to request that additional monitoring mechanisms are deployed at a provider's site is plausible and currently used in a variety of non-cloud systems.

8.4.2 Physical Data Location

Providers make business decisions on where to physically set up their data centers based on a number of parameters that may include construction costs, energy costs, safety and security concerns, availability of an educated work force, employee costs, and the quality of public infrastructure.

Consumers, however, may have to comply with international, Federal, or state statutes and directives that prohibit the storage of data outside certain physical boundaries or borders. Although technologists may have logical control over the data and employ cryptographic mechanisms to mitigate the risk of unauthorized disclosure, consumers must still comply with these statutes and regulations [NIST SP800-144].

8.4.3 Jurisdiction and Regulation

Consumers may be subjected to a variety of regulations such as the Sarbanes-Oxley Act (SOX), the Payment Card Industry Data Security Standard (PCI DSS), the Health Information Protection and Accountability Act (HIPAA), the Federal Information Security Management Act (FISMA) of 2002, or the Gramm-Leach-Bliley Act (GLBA). Consumers, who are ultimately responsible for their data processed on provider's systems, will need to require assurances from providers that they are aiding in compliance of the appropriate regulations.

Consumers also require assurance that appropriate legal jurisdiction exists for cloud services so that if providers fail to comply; legal remedies are understood in advance. These needs are complicated because providers typically view the implementation and configuration of their offerings as proprietary information, and do not offer consumers visibility into such details. This lack of visibility makes it difficult for consumers to be confident that providers are in compliance with regulations unless the provider obtains an independent audit from a trusted third party. Even here, the frequency of third party audits may limit the overall assurance offered, since a cloud system could quietly drift out of compliance, and continuous monitoring of cloud configurations and health may be desirable.

8.4.4 Support for Forensics

As part of an incident response effort, the goal of digital forensics is to: (1) discern what happened, (2) understand what portions of the system were affected, (3) learn how to prevent such incidents from happening again, and (4) collect information for possible future legal actions. Forensics in the cloud, however, raises a number of new issues, such as:

- How are incident handling responsibilities defined in service agreements? (see Appendix A)

- How are clocks synchronized across data centers to help reconstruct a chain of events?

- How are data breach notifications laws handled in different countries?

- What data can a cloud provider look at when capturing an image of a shared hard drive?

■ What is the consumer allowed to see in an audit log, e.g., is information related to other cloud consumers protected?

■ What is the responsibility of a consumer to report an incident in a PaaS model?

■ Can a provider legally intervene in stopping an attack on an application in its cloud if it is only an indirect contractual relationship (e.g., three tiers of customers)?

Forensic analysis in a SaaS model may be the sole responsibility of a provider while forensic analysis in an IaaS model may be the primary responsibility of the consumer (with some collaboration with the provider). The PaaS model appears to split responsibilities between consumers and providers.

8.5   Information Security

Information security pertains to protecting the confidentiality and integrity of data and ensuring data availability. An organization that owns and runs its IT operations will normally take the following types of measures for its data security:

■ Organizational/Administrative controls specifying who can perform data related operations such as creation, access, disclosure, transport, and destruction.

■ Physical Controls relating to protecting storage media and the facilities housing storage devices.

■ Technical Controls for Identity and Access Management (IAM), encryption of data at rest and in transit, and other data audit-handling requirements for complying with regulatory requirements.

When an organization subscribes to a cloud, all the data generated and processed will physically reside in premises owned and operated by a provider. In this context, the fundamental issue is whether a consumer can obtain an assurance that a provider is implementing the same or equivalent controls as to what the consumer would have implemented. The following issues arise when a consumer is trying to ensure coverage for these controls:

■ Regulatory compliance requirements, with regard to data that a consumer is intending to move to a cloud, may call for specific levels and granularities of audit logging, generation of alerts, activity reporting, and data retention. Since these may not be a part of standard service agreements offered by providers, the issue becomes whether consumers are willing to: (1) include these procedures as part of their contractual data protection responsibilities, and (2) enforce them as part of their standard operating procedures.

■ Even in cases where a provider meets the consumer's data protection requirements through contractual obligations and operational configurations, the provider should offer methods that the consumer can use to assess whether or not the requirements continue to be met.

■ For encryption of data at rest, the strength of the encryption algorithm suite, the key management schemes a provider supports, and the number of keys for each data owner (individual or shared keys) should be known by the data owners.

Data processed in a public cloud and applications running in a public cloud may experience different security exposures than would be the case in an onsite-hosted environment. A number of considerations affect security of data and processing conducted in a cloud. For example, the quality of a cloud's implementation, the attack surface of a cloud, the likely pool of attackers, system complexity, and the expertise level of cloud administrators are a few considerations that affect cloud system security.

Unfortunately, none of these considerations is decisive regarding cloud security and there are no obvious answers when comparing cloud to non-cloud systems as to which is likely to be more secure in practice. One aspect that is pervasive in cloud systems, however, is reliance on "logical separation", as opposed to "physical separation" of user workloads, and the use of logical mechanisms to protect consumer resources. Although more traditional systems employ logical separation also, they also employ physical separation (e.g., physically separated networks or systems) and logical separation has not been shown to be as reliable as physical separation; e.g. in the past, some virtualization systems have experienced failures under stress testing [Orm07]. The following subsections briefly describe some security issues; NIST SP 800-144 also discusses security issues for public clouds.

8.5.1   Risk of Unintended Data Disclosure

Unclassified government systems are often operated in a manner where a single system is used to process PII, FOUO, or proprietary information, as well as to process non-sensitive, public information. In a typical scenario, a user will store sensitive and nonsensitive information in separate directories on a system or in separate mail messages on an email server. By doing so, sensitive information is expected to be carefully managed to avoid unintended distribution. If a consumer wishes to use cloud computing for non-sensitive computing, while retaining the security advantages of on premises resources for sensitive computing, care must be taken to store sensitive data in encrypted form only.

8.5.2   Data Privacy

Privacy addresses the confidentiality of data for specific entities, such as consumers or others whose information is processed in a system. Privacy carries legal and liability concerns, and should be viewed not only as a technical challenge but also as a legal and ethical concern. Protecting privacy in any computing system is a technical challenge; in a cloud setting this challenge is complicated by the distributed nature of clouds and the possible lack of consumer awareness over where data is stored and who has or can have access.

8.5.3   System Integrity

Clouds require protection against intentional subversion or sabotage of the functionality of a cloud. Within a cloud there are stakeholders: consumers, providers, and a variety of administrators. The ability to partition access rights to each of these groups, while keeping malicious attacks at bay, is a key attribute of maintaining cloud integrity. In a cloud setting, any lack of visibility into a cloud's mechanisms makes it more difficult for consumers to check the integrity of cloud-hosted applications.

8.5.4   Multi-tenancy

Cloud computing receives significant economic efficiencies from the sharing of resources on the provider's side. For IaaS clouds, different VMs may share hardware via a hypervisor; for PaaS, different processes may share an operating system and supporting data and networking services; for SaaS, different consumers may share the same application or database.

Because the sharing mechanisms employed at a provider's facility depend on complex utilities to keep consumer workloads isolated, the risk of isolation failure exists. Flaws in logical separation have been documented in the past [Orm07].

Building confidence that logical separation is a suitable substitute for physical separation is a long-standing research problem, but the issue can be somewhat mitigated by encrypting data before entering it into a cloud. (Note that if the data is encrypted, it will need to be unencrypted to be processed.) For clouds that perform computations, mitigation can occur by limiting the kinds of data that are processed in the cloud or by contracting with providers for specialized isolation mechanisms such as the rental of entire computer systems rather than VMs (mono-tenancy), Virtual Private Networks (VPNs), segmented networks, or advanced access controls.

8.5.5 Browsers

Many cloud applications use the consumer's browser as a graphical interface. For example, a number of technologies (e.g., [Gar05, Ado11, Goo11-2, Mic11, Dja11]) allow consumer browsers to provide a cloud experience where the software "feels local" even though it runs in a cloud infrastructure. Although providers sometimes distribute client-side tools for cloud administration, browsers are also used for consumer account setup and resource administration, including the provisioning of financial information necessary to open and use an account with a provider. Unfortunately, browsers are complex, rivaling the complexity of early operating systems, and browsers have been shown to harbor security flaws and be vulnerable in nearly every public security challenge (e.g., [Por10, Mar09]). Providers interoperate with a diversity of consumer browsers and versions, and consumer-administered end systems and browsers may not be properly managed for security or may not be current. If a consumer's browser is subverted, all of the consumer's resources entrusted to a cloud provider are at risk.

Whenever browsers are the access points to a cloud, building confidence that browsers have not been subverted is important. Various approaches can be taken to build confidence, including accessing clouds from behind application gateway or network packet filtering firewalls, restricting the browser types that are approved for accessing a cloud, limiting browser plug-ins for browsers providing cloud access, ensuring that browsers are up-to-date, and locking down systems that access clouds via browsers. While practical and helpful, most of these techniques, however, raise costs, lower functionality, or reduce convenience.

8.5.6 Hardware Support for Trust

In some scenarios, hardware support can enable consumers to understand the trustworthiness of remote systems. As an example, a Trusted Platform Module (TPM)'s purpose is to store a set of checksums that are generated at system startup, and then attest when asked, that the system did in fact boot from known components. When virtual machines migrate, this would appear to weaken the trust chain in the TPM. Different groups have attempted to virtualize the TPM, or to construct an argument in which a re-awakened VM can reestablish trust on different hardware, but this issue remains open.

8.5.7 Key Management

Proper protection of consumer cryptographic keys appears to require some cooperation from cloud providers. The issue is that unlike dedicated hardware, zeroing a memory buffer may not delete a key if: (1) the memory is backed by a hypervisor that makes it persistent, (2) the VM is having a snapshot taken for recovery purposes, or (3) the VM is being serialized for migration to different hardware. It is an open issue on how to use cryptography safely from inside a cloud.

9. General Recommendations

For Federal information systems and those operated on behalf of the US Government, the Federal Information Security Management Act (FISMA) of 2002 and the associated NIST standards and special publications (e.g. FIPS 199, FIPS 200, SP 800-53 etc.) do apply to cloud systems. In the context of cloud computing, the following are additional general recommendations, broken into five groups for readability: Management, Data Governance, Security and Reliability, Virtual Machines, and Software and Applications.

9.1   Management

■ **Migrating Data to and from Clouds.** Consumers should identify the specific resources that are suitable for migrating data into and out of clouds. Resources could be services such as: (1) email, (2) data repositories such as shared documents, or (3) systems that run in virtualized environments. Consumers should develop a plan for both migrating the data to and from the cloud, and for interacting with the data once it is resident in the cloud. Consumers should plan also for an eventual termination of a provider's service during the procurement phase of the contract, and should clarify how assets are to be returned to consumers. Consumers should also plan for migration between clouds.

■ **Continuity of Operations.** If the cost of losing access to an application is severe, it is recommended that consumers perform the work locally unless a provider is willing to agree to pay for pre-defined damages for specific types of service interruptions. Consumers should review the provider's business continuity plan and redundancy architecture to understand if their stated availability goals are supported. Consumers should request assurances that a provider employs established internal operating procedures and service management techniques for reliable system updates, data transfers, and other site modifications. Consumers should consider that service agreements usually state that the provider will reimburse consumers for service outages by only refunding service fees, and not by compensating for actual damages arising from service interruptions. The level of availability of a cloud service and its capabilities for data backup and disaster recovery should be addressed in the organization's contingency and continuity plan to ensure the recovery and restoration of disrupted cloud services and operations, using alternate services, equipment, and locations, if required.

■ **Compliance.** A consumer should: (1) determine whether the capabilities for defining the necessary controls exist within a particular provider, (2) determine whether those controls are being implemented properly, and (3) ensure that the controls are documented. Traditional forms of direct assessment may not be feasible and may require working with the cloud provider to gain needed information and system access, or to allow third-party audits to establish a sufficient level of assurance. Also, a consumer should scrutinize any certifications (e.g., ISO 27001) or audit statements (e.g., SAS 70) available from the cloud provider for their scope of coverage and applicability.[15]

■ **Administrator Staff.** Consumers should make sure that processes are in place to compartmentalize the job responsibilities of the provider's administrators from the responsibilities of the consumer's administrators. The insider security threat is a well-known issue for most organizations and extends as well to the cloud provider's staff. Therefore, consumers should make sure that the cloud provider's policy, procedures, and controls to protect against malicious insiders are adequate.

---

[15] The Federal Risk and Authorization Management Program has been established to provide a standard approach, to assessing and authorizing cloud computing services, and products that results in a joint authorization of cloud providers with respect to a common security risk model. The joint authorization issued can be reused and leveraged across the Federal Government in cloud computing deployments for which the security risk model applies.

■ **Legal.** Consumers should investigate whether a provider can support ad hoc legal requests for: (1) e-Discovery, such as litigation freezes, and (2) preservation of data and meta-data.

■ **Operating Policies.** Consumers should ascertain the operating policies of providers for their: (1) willingness to be subjected to external audits and security certifications, (2) incident response and recovery procedures/practices, including forensic analysis capabilities, (3) internal investigation processes with respect to illegal or inappropriate usage of IT resources, and (4) policies for vetting of privileged uses such as the provider's system and network administrators.

■ **Acceptable Use Policies.** Consumers should ensure that all consumer personnel read and understand the provider's acceptable use policy, and negotiate an agreement for resolution of specific classes of policy violations in advance with the provider. Further, it is important that consumers know the process a priori for how disputes over possible policy violations will be resolved between themselves and the provider.

■ **Licensing.** Consumers should ensure that both the provider and consumer properly license any proprietary software installed into a cloud.

■ **Patch Management.** Consumers and providers should agree on a set of procedures a consumer needs to perform to take an application offline (whether a software patch is going to be installed by the provider or consumer), the testing that must be performed to ensure the application continues to perform as intended, and the procedures needed to bring the application back online. Plans for system maintenance should be expressed in the service agreement.

9.2 Data Governance

■ **Data Access Standards.** Before a decision is made to develop new applications in a cloud, consumers should ensure that the application infrastructure interfaces provided in that cloud are generic or at least that data adaptors could be developed so that portability and interoperability of the application is not significantly impacted. Consumers should choose clouds that work with well-documented data access protocols.

■ **Data Separation.** When data of differing levels of sensitivity are to be processed in a cloud, multiple distinct clouds can be used concurrently to provide different levels of protection to sensitive and nonsensitive data. When this approach is taken, protective mechanisms should be required by consumers for separating sensitive and nonsensitive data at the provider's site.

■ **Data Integrity.** Consumers should employ checksums and replication techniques for data integrity. Data can be protected from unauthorized modification in a cloud if it is check-summed and validated on use, and if the check-sums are stored separately.

■ **Data Regulations.** A consumer should assess the risks of having their data processed or stored in a cloud since the consumer is ultimately responsible for all compliances with data-related laws and regulations. Consumers should require that a cloud provider meet international, Federal, or state statutes and directives with which they must comply, e.g., that may prohibit the storage of data outside certain physical boundaries or borders.

■ **Data Disposition.** Consumers should require that a cloud provider offer a mechanism for reliably deleting consumer data on request as well as providing evidence that the data was deleted.

■ **Data Recovery.** Consumers should be able to examine the capabilities of providers with respect to: (1) data backup, (2) archiving, and (3) recovery.

9.3 Security and Reliability

■ **Consumer-Side Vulnerabilities.** Consumers should minimize the potential for web browsers or other client devices to be attacked by employing best practices for the security and hardening of consumer platforms, and should seek to minimize browser exposure to possibly malicious web sites.

■ **Encryption.** Consumers should require that strong (FIP 140-2 compliant) encryption be used for web sessions and other network communication whenever a rented application requires the confidentiality of application interactions with other applications or data transfers. Also consumers should require that the same diligence is applied to stored data.

■ **Physical.** Consumers should consider physical plant security practices and plans at provider sites as part of the overall risk considerations when selecting a provider. Physical attacks require backup plans just as cyber attacks do. Consumers should write plans for recovery from such attacks. Consumers should also investigate whether a candidate provider offers redundancy for the sites they operate, and opt for providers that are not tied to a specific geographic location in case of natural disasters or other disruptions.

■ **Authentication.** Consumers should consider the use of authentication tokens or other appropriate form of advanced authentication, which some providers offer, to mitigate the risk of account hijacking and other types of exploits.

■ **Identity and Access Management.** Consumers should have visibility into the following capabilities of a provider: (1) the authentication and access control mechanisms that the provider infrastructure supports, (2) the tools that are available for consumers to provision authentication information, and (3) the tools to input and maintain authorizations for consumer users and applications without the intervention of the provider.

■ **Performance Requirements.** Consumers should benchmark current performance scores for an application, and then establish key performance score requirements before deploying that application to a provider's site. Key performance scores include responsiveness for interactive user applications, and bulk data transfer performance for applications that must input or output large quantities of data on an ongoing basis.

■ **Visibility.** Consumers should request that a provider allow visibility into the operating services that affect a specific consumer's data or operations on that data, including monitoring of the system's welfare.

9.4 Virtual Machines

■ **VM Vulnerabilities.** When providers offer computing resources in the form of VMs, consumers should ensure that the provider has mechanisms to protect VMs from attacks by: (1) other VMs on the same physical host, (2) the physical host itself, and (3) the network. Typical attack detection and prevention mechanisms include Virtual Firewalls, Virtual IDS/IPS, and network segmentation techniques such as VLANs.

■ **VM Migration.** Consumers should formulate a strategy for migration of Virtual Machines and their associated storage among alternative cloud providers.

9.5 Software and Applications

■ **Time-critical Software.** Applications that require precise timing of task completion appear unsuitable for public and some outsourced cloud computing scenarios because of the variable response times that such systems may experience from unexpected and unavoidable round trip delays. Consumers should avoid using clouds for time-critical applications.

- **Safety-critical Software.** Because of the lack of ability to fully assess the "pedigree" for all subsystems composing a cloud, and because of network variability, employing cloud technologies for safety-critical applications at this time is not recommended.

- **Application Development Tools.** When available, consumers should choose clouds that provide application development frameworks that include an architecture and tools for mitigating security vulnerabilities. Tools that support the intuitive authoring and maintenance of security policies, and provide an integrated application development environment covering the full system lifecycle, with an orientation towards facilitating security accreditation, are preferable. Consumers should also assure that such tools satisfy as appropriate FIPS 140-2.

- **Application Runtime Support.** Before a decision is made to deploy a new application in a cloud, or in the case of composing an application from the building blocks offered by a provider, a consumer should ensure that libraries included in the compilation phase or libraries called during the execution phase behave as intended, both in terms of functionality and performance.

- **Application Configuration.** Consumers should ensure that an application can be configured to run in a secure manner (e.g., a dedicated VLAN segment) and can be integrated with existing enterprise/agency security frameworks (such as identification and authorization) such that enterprise/agency security policies are enforced.

- **Standard Programming Languages.** Consumers should choose clouds that work with standardized languages and tools wherever feasible.

Appendix A—Roles and Responsibilities

The partnership between providers and consumers in designing, building, deploying, and operating clouds presents new challenges in providing adequate security and privacy protection. It becomes a collaborative process between providers and consumers to share the responsibilities in implementing the necessary controls.

Cloud business models determine the ownership of the computing resources offered within a cloud. In the case of private clouds, where the provider is the same organizational entity as the consumer, discussions on the separations of responsibilities can still be helpful to the owner of a system deployed in a cloud. It can help that owner map out a comprehensive operational plan based on the collaboration between the logical roles of providers and consumers.

Thus clarity as to how to divide the roles and responsibilities of implementing security controls is important to help organizations: (1) define detailed security plans to address cloud security requirements, (2) develop or procure appropriate security measures during development, (3) objectively compare and evaluate providers, and (4) execute security protocols during the deployment and throughout operation. In addition, collaboration between providers and consumers can help ensure that clouds meet specific security conformance and regulatory requirements, especially for those supporting government agency operations.

This brief appendix discusses these issues by outlining the main technical security controls from NIST's Special Publication 800-53, and then suggests a roadmap for applying them to clouds by considering the patterns of different provider and consumer relationships for sharing security responsibilities.

The life cycle and life span of a system deployed in a cloud provides another perspective on how to delineate roles and responsibilities. The system developer and integrator are responsible for implementing security controls that need to be built into the system at development time. The system administrator and operator are responsible for implementing security controls that are executed at operation time.

For SaaS clouds, a provider may be both the developer/integrator and administrator/operator, and if so would normally assume most of the responsibility in implementing security controls. For IaaS clouds, a consumer typically assumes more responsibilities, since the consumer is not only the developer/integrator, but is also the administrator/operator. But a provider for IaaS clouds would still be responsible for providing protections at infrastructure levels that a consumer does not have control of. For PaaS clouds, a mixture of the two extremes occurs; while a consumer, as the developer/integrator, needs to build the necessary application level security controls into the system, a provider is responsible for providing all the system level protections. (A potential middle ground here involves third-party cloud security services. In this situation, responsibilities for providing protection to the entire system should be negotiated by all stakeholders.)

SP800-53 defines a comprehensive list of security controls for protecting IT systems. Each security control is either a capability deployed in a system, or a set of procedures or activities an organization carries out to implement security. SP800-53 also provides guidance on how to tailor the list of security controls to meet an organization's specific needs or accommodate a system's idiosyncrasies.

The security controls are organized into 17 families based on the domain areas of the security requirements. Further, as a starting point for consideration in assigning logical areas of responsibility for implementing security controls, the control families are grouped into three broad classes of management, technical and operational controls. Table 6 is a listing of the 17 families and the classes they belong to:

Table 2: 800-53 Control Families and Classes

Technical	Operational	Management
Access Control	Awareness and Training	Certification, Accreditation and Security Assessment
Audit and Accountability	Configuration and Management	Planning
Identification and Authentication	Contingency Planning	Risk Assessment
System and Communication Protection	Incident Response	System and Services Acquisition
	Maintenance	
	Media Protection	
	Physical and Environmental Protection	
	Personnel Security	
	System and Information Integrity	

The current NIST baselines in SP800-53 are a starting point for cloud applications and services as well as for the information systems that are providing those applications and services. SP800-53 offers tailoring guidance that allows adjustments for cloud computing environments. Additional guidance will be required at lower levels of abstraction as the current security controls in SP800-53 are written to be technology and policy neutral.

Currently work is being undertaken to develop additional guidance. The following three key observations are included in those findings:

- Policy and procedure related technical security controls are typically a consumer's responsibility. Providers will likely offer input as to the feasibility and cost of enforcing these policies and procedures, especially if the provider has the responsibilities to implement them. System capability-related controls are the responsibility of the capability developer at build time or the administrator during operation. For example, account management controls for privileged users in an IaaS cloud are typically performed by the IaaS provider, whereas account management for user and application consumers of an application deployed in an IaaS environment is typically not the provider's responsibility. The consumer's organization is often fully responsible for managing the accounts, unless the consumer outsources the responsibility to a third-party ID management broker.

- Operational families of security controls are about policies, procedures, and processes. A consumer is typically responsible for the definitions and the provider shares responsibilities during execution (since the provider is an operational partner). However, the nature of the cooperation will affect the extent of the applicability of these controls; for example, a provider would need to be definitive as to whether regularly held security training is required or is feasible for their staff. These operational security controls form a checklist when a consumer is comparison-shopping for a provider as well as during service agreement negotiations.

- The four management class security control families mentioned in Table 6 are similar to operational class security controls and are the responsibility of a consumer. The provider plays a supporting role here to help the consumer by offering necessary documentation and evidence to meet these requirements. It is possible that some providers may alter their own business process and technical solutions to fulfill some of the security management requirements from the consumer.

Appendix B—Acronyms

Selected acronyms and abbreviations used in the guide are defined below.

AJAX	group of Web development methods
API	Application Programming Interface
CPU	Computer Processing Unit
DBMS	Database Management System
DNS	Domain Name Server
FISMA	Federal Information Security Management Act
HTML	Hypertext Markup Language
HTTP	Hypertext Transfer Protocol
HTTPS	Hypertext Transfer Protocol Secure
IaaS	Infrastructure as a Service
IDS/IPS	Intrusion Detection Systems/Intrusion Prevention Systems
ISO	International Standards Organization
IT	Information Technology
ITL	Information Technology Laboratory
IA-64	64-bit Intel Itanium architecture
IP	Internet Protocol
JVM	Java Virtual Machine
NIST	US National Institute of Standards and Technology
PaaS	Platform as a Service
OMB	Office of Management and Budget
OVF	Open Virtualization Format
PEM	Privacy Enhanced Mail
SaaS	Software as a Service

SP	Special Publication
SQL	Structured Query Language
SSL/TLS	Secure Socket Layer/Transport Layer Security
TCP	Transmission Control Protocol
VLAN	Virtual Local Area Network
VM	Virtual Machine
VMM	Virtual Machine Monitor
VPN	Virtual Private Networks
VRF	VPN Routing and Forwarding
WSDL	Web Services Description Language
XML	Extensible Markup Language

Appendix C—Glossary

Selected terms used in the publication are defined below.

Authentication: Verifying the identity of a user, process, or device, often as a prerequisite to allowing access to resources in an information system.

Certificate: A digital representation of information which at least: (1) identifies the certification authority issuing it, (2) names or identifies its consumer, (3) contains the consumer's public key, (4) identifies its operational period, and (5) is digitally signed by the certification authority issuing it.

Compliance: Conformity in fulfilling official requirements.

IaaS: Defined in the NIST Cloud Computing Definition, excerpted in Section 2.

PaaS: Defined in the NIST Cloud Computing Definition, excerpted in Section 2.

Public key cryptography: An encryption method that uses a two-part key: a public key and a private key. Users generally distribute their public key, but keep their private key to themselves. This is also known as "Asymmetric Cryptography."

SaaS: Defined in the NIST Cloud Computing Definition, excerpted in Section 2.

Service agreement: A legal document specifying the rules of the legal contract between the cloud user and the cloud provider.

Service-level agreement: A document stating the technical performance promises made by the cloud provider, how disputes are to be discovered and handled, and any remedies for performance failures.

Virtual machine (VM): "an efficient, isolated duplicate of a real machine" [Pop74].

Virtualization: "The simulation of the software and/or hardware upon which other software runs" [NIST SP 800-125].

Appendix D—References

The lists below provide examples of resources that may be helpful.

[Ado11]   Adobe Systems Inc., "Adobe Flex Framework Technologies", 2011, http://labs.adobe.com/technologies/flex.

[Ama06]   Amazon Web Services, "Amazon Simple Storage Service API Reference," Copyright @ 2010 Amazon Web Services LLC or its affiliates, http://awsdocs.s3.amazonaws.com/S3/latest/s3-api.pdf.

[Ama10]   Amazon Web Services, "Amazon Elastic Compute Cloud API Reference API Version 2010-11-15", 2010, http://aws.amazon.com/documentation/ec2.

[Ama12]   Amazon Web Services, "Amazon Elastic Beanstalk," Copyright @ 2012 Amazon Web Services LLC or its affiliates, http://aws.amazon.com/elasticbeanstalk.

[Can11]   Canonical Ltd., Bazaar branches of Eucalyptus (source code), 2011, [Online] https://code.launchpad.net/eucalyptus.

[Cha06]   Fay Chang, Jeffrey Dean, Sanjay Ghemawat, Wilson C. Hsieh, Deborah A. Wallach, Mike Burrows., Tushar Chandra, Andrew Fikes, Robert E. Gruber, "Bigtable: A Distributed Storage System for Structured Data," 2006, Proceedings of the 7th USENIX Symposium on Operating Systems Design and Implementation, Nov. 6-8, Seattle, WA.

[Che94]   William R. Cheswick, Steven M. Bellovin, "Firewalls and Internet Security: Repelling the Wily Hacker," 1994, Addison-Wesley, ISBN B000OOQ4R0.

[Chr05]   Christopher Clark, Keir Fraser, Steven Hand, Jacob Gorm Hansen, Eric Jul, Christian Limpach, Ian Pratt, Andrew Warfield, "Live Migration of Virtual Machines," Proceedings of the 2nd Symposium on Networked Systems Design and Implementation, May 2-4, 2005, Boston MA.

[Cho06]   Frederick Chong and Gianpaolo Carraro, "Architecture Strategies for Catching the Long Tail," Microsoft Corporation, April 2006. http://msdn.microsoft.com/en-us/library/aa479069.aspx.

[Com88]   Douglas Comer, "Internetworking with TCP/IP Principles, Protocols, and Architectures," Prentice-Hall, Inc., 1988, ISBN 0-13-470154-2.

[Dea04]   Jeffrey Dean and Sanjay Ghemawat, "MapReduce: Simplified Data Processing on Large Clusters," Proceedings of the 6'th USENIX Symposium on Operating Systems Design and Implementation, Dec. 6-8, 2004, San Francisco, CA.

[Die08]   T. Dierks and E. Rescorla, "The Transport Layer Security (TLS) Protocol Version 1.2," 2008, IETF RFC 5246, http://www.ietf.org/rfc/rfc5246.txt.

[Dja11]   Django Software Foundation, "django The Web framework for perfectionists with deadlines," 2011, http://www.djangoproject.com.

[DMT09]   Distributed Management Task Force, "Open Virtualization Format Specification, Version 1.0.0", 2009, online: http://www.dmtf.org/sites/default/files/standards/documents/DSP0243_1.0.0.pdf.

[Eps99]   Jeremy Epstein, "Architecture and Concepts of the ARGuE Guard," Proceedings of the 1999 Annual Computer Security Applications Conference, Dec. 6-10, 1999, Phoenix, Arizona.

[Fed10]   CIO Council, "Proposed Security Assessment and Authorization for U.S. Government Cloud Computing, Draft version 0.96, Nov. 2010. Online: www.FedRAMP.gov.

[Fer92]   David F. Ferraiolo and D.R. Kuhn, "Role Based Access Control," Proceedings of the 15th National Computer Security Conference, Oct 13-16, 1992, pp. 554-563.

[Gar05]   Jesse James Garrett, "Ajax: A New Approach to Web Applications," 2005, http://www.adaptivepath.com/ideas/essays/archives/000385.php.

[Gas88]   Morrie Gasser, "Building a Secure Computer System," 1988, Van Nostrand Reinhold Company Inc., ISBN 0-442-23022-2.

[Ghe03]   Sanjay Ghemawat, Howard Gobioff, and Shun-Tak Leung, "The Google File System," SOSP '03, Oct 19-22, 2003, Bolton Landing, New York, USA.

[Goo11]   Google, "Google App Engine", Copyright 2011 Google, http://code.google.com/appengine.

[Goo11-2]   Google, "Google Web Toolkit", Copyright 2011, http://code.google.com/Webtoolkit.

[ISO/IEC 23271:2006] Information technology -- Common Language Infrastructure (CLI) Partitions I to VI, 2006, JTC1/SC22, online: http://standards.iso.org/ittf/PubliclyAvailableStandards/index.html.

[Kar09]   A. H. Karp, H. Haury, and M. H. Davis, "From ABAC to ZBAC: the Evolution of Access Control Models," Tech. Report HPL-2009-30, HP Labs, Feb. 21, 2009, http://www.hpl.hp.com/techreports/2009/HPL-2009-30.pdf.

[Lind99]   Tim Linkholm and Frank Yellin, "The Java Virtual Machine Specification Second Edition," 1999, online, http://java.sun.com/docs/books/jvms/second_edition/html/VMSpecTOC.doc.html.

[Mar09]   Moxie Marlinspike, "New Tricks for Defeating SSL In Practice," 2009, http://www.blackhat.com/presentations/bh-dc-09/Marlinspike/BlackHat-DC-09-Marlinspike-Defeating-SSL.pdf.

[Mat08]   Jeanna N. Matthews, Eli M. Dow, Todd Deshane, Wenjin Hu, Jeremy Bongio, Patrick F. Wilbur, Brendan Johnson, "Running Xen a Hands-On Guide to the Art of Virtualization," Pearson Education, Inc., 2008, ISBN-13: 978-0-132-34966-6.

[Mic10]   Microsoft, "Hyper-V: Using Live Migration with Cluster Shared Volumes in Windows Server 208 R2," Microsoft TechNet August 25, 2010. http://technet.microsoft.com/en-us/library/dd446679(WS.10).aspx.

[Mic11]   Microsoft, "Microsoft Silverlight," 2011, http://www.microsoft.com/silverlight.

[Moc87-1]   Paul Mockapetris, "Domain Names - Concepts and Facilities," IETF RFC 1034, 1987, http://tools.ietf.org/html/rfc1034.

[Moc87-2]   Paul Mockapetris, "Domain Names - Implementation and Specification," IETF RFC 1035, 1987, http://tools.ietf.org/html/rfc1035.

[Mos05]   Tim Moses, "eXtensible Access Control Markup Language (XACML) Version 2.0," OASIS Standard, Feb. 1, 2005, http://docs.oasis-open.org/xacml/2.0/access_control-xacml-2.0-core-spec-os.pdf.

[Msf11]   Microsoft, "Windows Azure Storage Services REST API Reference," Copyright 2011 Microsoft, http://msdn.microsoft.com/en-us/library/dd179355.aspx.

[Msf11-2]   Microsoft, "Windows Azure," Copyright 2011 Microsoft, http://msdn.microsoft.com/en-us/library/dd179367.aspx.

[Nas10]   NASA Nebula IaaS Team, "NASA Nebula IaaS", 2010, [Online] http://nebula.nasa.gov.

[Net96]   Netscape, "The SSL Protocol: Version 3.0," Netscape/Mozilla, [Online] 1996. http://www.mozilla.org/projects/security/pki/nss/ssl/draft302.txt.

[Nur08]   Nurmi, Daniel, Rich Wolski, Chris Grzegorczyk, Graziano Obertelli, Sunil Soman, Lamia Youseff, Dmitrii Zagorodnov, "The Eucalyptus Open-source Cloud-computing System," in Proceedings of the 2009 IEEE/ACM International Symposium on Cluster Computing and the Grid, May 2009.

[Nur08-2]   Nurmi, Daniel, Rich Wolski, Chris Grzegorczyk, Graziano Obertelli, Sunil Soman, Lamia Youseff, Dmitrii Zagorodnov, "Eucalyptus A technical report on an elastic utility computing architecture linking your programs to useful systems," UCSB Technical Report, 2008-10.

[Oid11]   The OpenID Foundation, "OpenID," 2011, http://openid.net.

[Oix10]   Open Identity Exchange, "An Open Market Solution for Online Identity Assurance," Copyright 2010 OIX Corporation, http://openidentityexchange.org/sites/default/files/oix-white-paper-2010-03-02.pdf.

[Opp03]   David Oppenheimer, Archana Ganapathi, and David A. Patterson, "Why do Internet services fail, and what can be done about it?" Proceedings of the 4th Usenix Symposium on Internet Technologies and Systems, 2003.

[Orm07]   T. Ormandy, "An Empirical Study into the Security Exposure to Hosts of Hostile Virtualized Environments," CanSecWest, 2007, Vancouver, British Columbia.

[Per08]   R. Perez, L. van Doorn, R. Sailer, "Virtualization and Hardware-Based Security,"
            Security and Privacy, IEEE , vol.6, no.5, pp.24-31, Sept.-Oct. 2008; URL:
            http://ieeexplore.ieee.org/stamp/stamp.jsp?tp=&arnumber=4639019&isnumber=4639007

[Pop74]   Gerald Popek and Robert Goldberg, "Formal Requirements for Virtualizable Third
            Generation Architectures," July 1974, Communications of the ACM, Vol. 17.

[Por10]   Aaron Portnoy, "Pwn2Own2010", 2010, TippingPoint Digital Vaccine Laboratories,
            online: http://dvlabs.tippingpoint.com/blog/2010/02/15/pwn2own-2010.

[Pyt11]   Python Software Foundation, "Extending and Embedding the Python Interpreter,"
            copyright 2011, The Python Software Foundation, online,
            http://docs.python.org/py3k/extending/index.html#extending-index.

[Rag08]   N. Ragouzis et al., "Security Assertion Markup Language (SAML) V2.0 Technical
            Overview," OASIS Committee Draft, March 2008, http://www.oasis-
            open.org/committees/download.php/27819/sstc-saml-tech-overview-2.0-cd-02.pdf.

[Ran99]   Marcus Ranum, "Installing the Trusted Information Systems Internet Firewall Toolkit,"
            1996, http://www.fwtk.org/fwtk/docs/mjr-slides.

[Red10]   Redhat, "RED HAT PaaS: Bringing open choice & application portability to the cloud,"
            2010, http://www.jboss.com/pdf/RedHatPaaSWhitepaper.pdf.

[Red99]   Redhat Emerging Technology, "KVM Migration," last updated: June 2009,
            http://www.linux-kvm.org/page/Migration.

[Ros99]   E. Rosen, Y. Rekhter, "BGP/MPLS VPNs," IETF RFC 2547, 1999,
            http://www.ietf.org/rfc/rfc2547.txt.

[Sal11]   salesforce, "Force.com," copyright 2011 salesforce.com,
            http://www.salesforce.com/platform.

[Sch94]   Bruce Schneier, "Applied Cryptography," John Wiley and Sons, Inc., 1994, ISBN 0-471-
            59756-2.

[Shr10]   Gautam. Shroff, "Enterprise Cloud Computing Technology, Architecture, Applications,"
            Cambridge University Press, 2010, ISBN 978-0-521-76095-9.

[Sii01]   Software and Information Industry Association, "Strategic Backgrounder: Software as a
            Service," 2001, [Online] http://www.siia.net/estore/pubs/SSB-01.pdf.

[SNI09]   SNIA, "Cloud Storage Use Cases Version 0.5 rev 0," Trial-Use Draft, Copyright 2009
            Storage Networking Industry Association,
            http://www.snia.org/tech_activities/publicreview/CloudStorageUseCasesv0.5.pdf.

[SNI10]   SNIA, "Cloud Data Management Interface Version 1.1f," Work In Progress, Copyright
            2010 Storage Networking Industry Association,
            http://www.snia.org/tech_activities/publicreview/CDMI_Spec_v1.01f_DRAFT.pdf.

[TIS94]   Trusted Information Systems, "TIS Firewall Toolkit," June 30, 1994, http://www.fwtk.org/fwtk/docs/overview.pdf.

[Vmw11]   VMware, "VMware vSphere VMWARE VMOTIONTM Migrate Virtual Machines with Zero Downtime," 2011, http://www.vmware.com/products/vmotion.

[War09]   Simon Wardley, Etienne Goyer and Nick Barcet, "Ubuntu Enterprise Cloud Architecture," 2009, online: http://www.canonical.com/sites/default/files/active/Whitepaper-UbuntuEnterpriseCloudArchitecture-v1.pdf.

[Ylo06]   T. Ylonen and C. Lonvick, "The Secure Shell (SSH) Protocol Architecture," 2006, IETF RFC 4251, http://www.ietf.org/rfc/rfc4251.txt.

[Zwi00]   Elizabeth D. Zwicky, Simon Cooper, and D. Brent Chapman, "Building Internet Firewalls," 2000 O'Reilly and Associates, Inc. ISBN 1-56592-871-7.

Appendix E—NIST Publications

NIST 800 Series Special Publications are available at:
http://csrc.nist.gov/publications/nistpubs/index.html.

NIST FIPS Publications are available at: http://csrc.nist.gov/publications/PubsFIPS.html.

[SP 800-41]   NIST Special Publication 800-41, Revision 1, *Guidelines on Firewalls and Firewall Policy*, September 2009.

[SP 800-53]   NIST Special Publication 800-53, Revision 3, *Recommended Security Controls for Federal Information Systems and Organizations*, May 1, 2010, DOC.

[SP 800-63]   NIST Special Publication 800-63, *Electronic Authentication Guideline*, April 2006.

[SP 800-125]   NIST Special Publication 800-125, *Guide to Security for Full Virtualization Technologies*, January 2011.

[SP 800-144]   NIST Special Publication 800-144, *Guidelines on Security and Privacy in Public Cloud Computing*, November 2011.

[SP 800-145]   NIST Special Publication 800-145, *The NIST Definition of Cloud Computing,* September 2011.

[FIPS 200]   NIST FIPS 200, *Minimum Security Requirements for Federal Information and Information Systems*, March 2006, DOC.

[FIPS 199]   NIST FIPS 199, *Standards for Security Categorization of Federal Information and Information Systems*, February 2004, DOC.

[FIPS 140]   NIST FIPS 140-2, *Security Requirements for Cryptographic Modules*, December 2002, DOC.